MW00929478

Dear   2/14/08

Happy Valentine's Day!
Happy Vatenes Day!

We love our Savior Jesus Christ and
Weloesous Sunan Joearcnes

the gospel.
The gapes.

      We watched the funeral of
      We wancee the fulenn of

President Hinckley. A friend made
Deaden e flinckeg

a copy for us.

      We are thankful for and pray
      We ar tnakuf for and pay

for our new church presidency.
f on our nowe cheacn padeso gaug

      The leadership broadcast about
      The aacmewsnae beabacan obyt

raising a righteous posterity stressed
etfng an nana paug y stead

7-14 (read scriptures all 7 days + pray twice
7M Good sad to all 7dav tan bcm

each of 7 days) and family home evening.
Baicnas dan antcong bccmaaug

We miss you. May God Bless you. Love
Wang MgGodBuggLae
DonnAgrenn

The Broken Toy

A Story of a Fragile X Syndrome Child

By

Marilyn Morgan

authorHOUSE™

1663 LIBERTY DRIVE, SUITE 200
BLOOMINGTON, INDIANA 47403
(800) 839-8640
WWW.AUTHORHOUSE.COM

First published by AuthorHouse 04/20/05

ISBN: 1-4208-2950-5 (sc)

Library of Congress Control Number: 2005900930

Printed in the United States of America
Bloomington, Indiana

This book is printed on acid-free paper.

Table of Contents

Once we determined Jem would be k,
I packed for my Calif trip while Cheri called
dad for directions to the Phoenix Greyhound
Station. Cheri, Mary, John + James drove me
there. I got my ticket for the 10pm bus. It
was full so I & 10 other people were left
behind. We thought we'd have to wait 2½
hrs for the next bus. At 11:00 they gave
us our own bus express w/ only 1 stop

Broken Toy

My brother Danny is mentally retarded. For most of his life, he has been at a lower mental ability than I have been. I am three years younger than him; yet act as if I were ten years older! By the time I was talking in complete sentences, I was taking care of Danny. For as long as I can remember, I've felt the obligation to watch out for Dan. The principal of my elementary school successfully persuaded me to respect and appreciate my brother for who he is. In a way, this lesson was the biggest and most difficult step to cross.

A few months ago, a friend of mine asked what's it like to have a brother who is eighteen, and has the mental ability of a third grader? Since there is no possible way for me to express the pain, anger, excitement, and love I experienced with Dan, I thought for a moment.

How could I have explained the feeling of sorrow I had since Dan rarely or never said he loved me, and always addressed me by a swear word, not knowing any better? At night, saying, "I love you Dan", and getting the response, "Me too, NOT!" Every time he said that, it was like someone slammed a spike through my heart.

How could I have expressed the joy knowing I've been blessed with the responsibility of this glorious soul? Influencing my interests and values so greatly, it's incomprehensible.

"It's like receiving a toy," I said, "acquiring a broken toy. A toy which you've waited you're entire life for, and you treasure that toy, as if it's a part of you. Disregarding the faults of the toy, you cherish that toy as if nothing was wrong with it. Loving it more and more every day that you played with it".

Until recently, there have been no consequences or problems with being my brother's keeper. When Danny came to my elementary school for two years, I stood up for him if anyone bothered him. I even stepped up to this really "tough" jerk, Dan's age, and said; "if there's anything you have to say about Dan, say it to me". It's a good thing that he walked away, because that guy would have pounded my head in. Then, before I knew what had happened, Dan finally came to the realization that he's three years older than me and he should be taking care of me! This was a fatal blow. It took me a long, long time to accept the fact that he didn't need me anymore. I had been his crutch, and now, he is able to walk all by himself. This is just another step of the stairway.

Bob Morgan 1995

Dedication

I dedicate this book to my husband Mike. It is through his love and encouragement that enabled me to complete this book. His acceptance and sense of humor during Danny's difficult developmental years, as well as his belief that we can provide the best quality of life for our son, enabled Danny to become the happy independent young man he is today.

Acknowledgements

Conquer Fragile X Inc.
450 Royal Palm Way, Suite 400
Palm Beach, FL 33480
Telephone 561-842-9219
Fax: 877-275-1192
E-Mail: mail@cfxf.org
Website: http://www.cfxf.org

FRAXA
45 Pleasant St.
Newburyport, MA. 01950
Phone: (978) 462-1866
Fax: (978) 463-9985
E-Mail: info@fraxa.org
Website: http://www.fraxa.org

National Fragile X Foundation
P.O. Box 190488
San Francisco, CA 94119-0488
Phone 1: (800)-688-8765
Fax: (925) 938-9315
E-Mail: NATLFX@FragileX.org
Website: http://www.FragileX.org

Introduction

If only someone would have told me how everything would turn out and been able to predict the future of my son's life I could have relaxed. If only I had known what a wonderful young man Dan would become, the anxiety I felt would have lessened. The dilemma was that no one knew and no predictions were made about Danny's abilities and future life.

I kept the scariest possibilities hidden and unspoken to all that met us, including my closest family and friends. The thought that Daniel might not develop or progress at all was always on my mind. Since there was no group that Dan fit into, and no one able to suggest the direction to take with and for him, I was left to push, teach, and try to convince others and myself that Dan had a future filled with endless possibilities. After all, he was born with the same abilities, wasn't he? He was just behind and would soon catch up, wouldn't he? These are the questions that I constantly asked myself. As time went on I wondered if I or anyone else would be able to or want to answer those very questions.

When your baby is born you feel the surge of joy and hope that your child will be the next great doctor, lawyer, scientist, president, or other successful and famous person. The very least that you imagine is that he or she will solve some of the world's problems, and of course contribute to society. How then can you reconcile this with the reality that your child might be retarded? I, for one, was in denial and that was my way of dealing with the difficult situation.

Raising a child is not comparable to following a cookbook recipe, and many variables will affect the outcome. Still, we know each parent's in-put molds the outcome of a child's development. I am therefore hopeful that our life experiences will help each and every parent searching for assistance in raising their special needs child.

If only I had known Danny had FragileX Syndrome, the assistance I would have received from experts in the field would have enabled me to expand upon my knowledge that was acquired only through a lifetime of trial and error. The information available now at the click of a mouse or a trip to the library was unavailable to me. The resources are there today and I encourage you to avail yourself of every opportunity to gain as much knowledge as possible to aid in the development of your special needs child.

As you will read in the subsequent chapters I did not come to terms with his limitations until much later. I instead focused all of my energies on his progress and working with him on a daily basis. I now believe that it was this mindset that allowed for his success.

Chapter One:
Fragile X

"Fragile X syndrome is an X-linked hereditary condition affecting cognitive, physical, and sensory development. Fragile X syndrome is the most common inherited cause of mental retardation. It is second only to Down's syndrome as a cause of mental retardation. It is estimated that 1 in 259 people carry the gene and that one in 2,000 males are affected by it. Approximately 1 in 2,000 females are affected. Since males have only one X chromosome, they are affected more frequently and severely than females."[1]

Fragile X syndrome occurs in all ethnic, racial and socio-economic backgrounds. It is an X-linked genetic mutation that involves unstable trinucleotoids repeats CGG found near the tip of the X chromosome. Normal individuals have approximately 10 to 50 repeats while affected people have 200 to 2000 repeats. There cannot be father to son inheritance; this is because fathers pass a Y chromosome to their sons and an X chromosome to their daughters. Fathers carrying the Fragile X gene pass it to their daughters. Mothers carrying the Fragile X gene have a 50-50 chance of passing it to their sons or daughters. About 20% of male carriers of the Fragile X gene are totally unaffected.

"Detailed Description Of The FMR-1 Gene

1. The FMR-1 gene is located on the X chromosome. This gene is responsible for instructing the cell to make FMRP, a protein assumed to be essential for normal brain functioning.

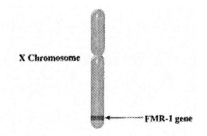

2. The genetic code for the FMR-1 gene usually contains a limited repetition of CGG sequences. The normal range is 5-50 repeats.

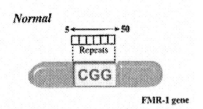

3. Some people have an expanded number of CGG repeats. When the number of CGG repeats is between 50 and 200 the individual Is a premutation carrier of fragile X syndrome. Carriers are not usually affected by fragile X syndrome, but they are at risk of having affected children.

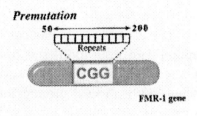

4. If the number of repeats exceeds 200, usually this disrupts the code and prevents the production of the FMR protein. These individuals have the full mutation and usually are affected by Fragile X syndrome.

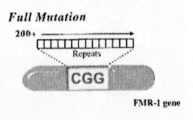

The Effects Of Fragile X

Fragile X is the leading form of autism of known cause: 90% of Fragile X patients have autistic features, 50% of pre-school Fragile X children meet autism diagnostic criteria, and 6% of all autistic individuals turn out to have Fragile X. Fragile X also gives rise to anxiety disorders, attention deficit hyperactivity disorder, psychosis, obsessive-compulsive disorder, and many other problems."[2]

"Individuals carrying the Fragile X chromosome vary widely in the degree they are affected. Physical characteristics may include low muscle tone, frequent ear infections, loose joints, long faces, prominent ears and large testicles. Behavioral characteristics may include speech and language delay, ADHD, sensory integration dysfunction, over and under responsiveness to sights, sounds, smells and touch; autistic-like characteristics, hand flapping, finger biting, poor eye contact and preservative speech."[3]

"Is There a Cure for Fragile X Syndrome?

There is currently no cure for Fragile X Syndrome, although appropriate education and medications can help maximize the potential of each child. However, most boys and many girls remain significantly affected throughout their lives. The cost to society for treatment, special education, and lost income is staggering. The need for research aimed at treatment is urgent. Recent significant progress has been made in understanding mechanisms and developing potential treatments for inherited diseases that are caused by a single gene, such as Fragile X. Current medical research focuses on:

Gene Therapy - studying the gene that causes Fragile X in order to determine whether a healthy gene may be inserted into the cells of affected individuals, thereby replacing the mutated, ineffective gene.

Protein Replacement Therapy - studying the protein product that is lacking due to the mutation, in hopes that the protein may be supplemented from an external source.

Psychopharmacology - treating the symptoms of the disorder with medications."[4]

Many researchers believe that medical treatment, when it becomes available, will be able to help Fragile X individuals of all ages. Experts think that the missing FMR protein has a regulatory function in the brain.

Chapter Two:
The Adventure Begins

I was teaching seventh grade in Chicago in 1977 in an inner city school. I loved my job. Before I went on maternity leave, I was afraid of becoming bored at home. My delivery date was November first, so I opted to go back to work in September, planning to work as long as I was able. I attended Lamaze classes weekly and continued teaching. The only problem I encountered was being unable to drive because I couldn't reach the accelerator or brake pedals. My stomach protruded so far in front that I had to move the seat all the way back in order to fit into the drivers seat. I was unable to drive because of my short legs not reaching the pedals. We solved that dilemma by having my husband drive me to and from work since he taught nearby. No one could tell that I was pregnant from the back. I was carrying totally in front, and except for the kicking to my ribs, my aversion to seafood, and not being able to drive in my ninth month, my pregnancy was not only uneventful, but also normal and fun.

I experienced false labor two weeks before I delivered and was kept overnight for observation. At my doctor's suggestion, I moved into my parent's condominium. They resided in Chicago and were much closer to the hospital. We lived an hour away, and were determined to use our favorite family gynecologist and not be forced to deliver at a local hospital. Two weeks later, I arrived at the hospital again, this time, to deliver my first-born.

On October 26,1977 Daniel Howard Morgan was born to the proud parents Michael and Marilyn. It was a long and difficult delivery, but Danny was, we thought, a perfect baby.

Danny didn't open his eyes for the first two days, but was declared a healthy baby, weighing in at eight and a half pounds and measuring 21 inches. He was beautiful. He did spit up a lot, but we had no clue that he would have anything but a perfectly happy and healthy life. In the seventies women were encouraged to stay in the hospital after giving birth and since Danny was slightly jaundiced we stayed for five days. He never needed any treatment for his jaundice.

His digestive tract was the first warning of significant and serious problems to come. After arriving home Danny began having continual bowel movements. The pediatrician advised us to change formula since he probably suffered from allergies. We went through every available formula and the problem only got worse. Now he began experiencing diarrhea and he was losing weight. At first, I was told that it was normal for an infant to lose weight after leaving the hospital but Danny had other problems as well, and his stomach ailments quickly worsened. It seemed like no one had a solution. During Danny's first two months of life, we tried every formula available on the shelf, as well as some special order ones without success, or relief for our suffering infant.

Every day I gave Dan a bath. He loved the water, but when I dried him, he would begin screaming. He did not stop until he was totally dressed, swaddled in a blanket and fed his bottle. This was the only time I was able to hold him, rock him and feel that I was able to relieve his pain and misery. Otherwise, my holding him did not afford him any comfort. When I asked about this, neither family member nor doctors were able to suggest anything beside colic. I accepted this, but continued to have an uneasy intuitive feeling that something else was wrong.

At three months, Danny was admitted into a local hospital where he was put in the diarrhea ward with other infants suffering from this continual problem. He was diagnosed as "failure to thrive,"₅ and was no better when he was discharged than when he was admitted. His diagnosis referred to his inability to gain weight. We tried feeding him cereal, and feeding him in an upright position, but now in addition to diarrhea he suffered from projectile vomiting₆. Our pediatrician instructed me to call him on a daily basis to check on his progress and each day he suggested something new. He never gave up hope or let a day go by that he didn't offer some word of encouragement. He felt that with the passage of time Danny's stomach problems would subside. Our pediatrician was on staff at a Chicago Hospital and assured me he would refer him for admission there for additional tests if he did not experience significant improvement.

Sleeping through the night was not a problem for Danny after the first three months. Every night, Danny fell asleep at eight o'clock and his Dad would wake him for a bottle of formula at eleven. We continued preparing formula until Danny was three years old. Each morning, he would sleep a little longer, until he slept through the night, not waking until five a.m. We discovered that we could steal one extra hour of sleep by placing him in his swing. Our swing had a cradle to lie down flat in, and could be wound for an hour of rocking movement.

7

The minute the swing stopped, he would awaken screaming. This routine enabled me to acquire enough sleep to manage the trials and tribulations of the day. Danny also napped for two hours between eleven and one during the day. He continued these sleeping habits until he was five years old.

I had not begun to worry about his developmental delays because we were too worried about his survival. At five months of age, Danny was admitted to a Chicago hospital for evaluation. They ruled out many terrible diseases and suggested pre-digested formula. We sat in the waiting room terrified reading numerous brochures describing Tay Sachs$_7$ and other diseases Danny was being tested for. These tests proved to be negative, but the Doctor's were unable to diagnose what he did have. We were looking for answers but the ones available could have proven fatal.

It was believed that Danny's developmental delays were directly tied to his "failure to thrive." Doctors believed that lack of weight gain did not allow him to physically have the necessary strength for developmental gains.

One week later, as we entered the hospital we saw a malnourished and sickly baby in a walker that looked close to death. To our horror, we discovered as we walked closer that it was Danny. His one side of his face was flat and after many Doctor's examinations and tests they determined that this was self-inflicted by favoring and lying only on one side when he slept. He still did not respond when we tried to cuddle with him and now we told ourselves that must be because of the stomach pain. He was still experiencing diarrhea and projectile vomiting.

During this time Dan was unable to turn over by himself. He had flipped a number of times when he was three months by turning his head and then twisting his little body until he turned. This did not continue, we suspected, because he was weak from lack of nutrition. However, he did not pick himself up by his arms and rock, or begin to attempt a crawling position. We were very aware that this was a serious developmental delay.

During Danny's hospital stay, a wonderful neurologist who we still see today first diagnosed him. The results of his first EEG$_8$ were positive. When he was retested the results were negative. So, even though the results were inconclusive, Epilepsy$_9$ was suspected. Originally, the reason for these tests was that Danny was turning blue around the mouth while he was drinking his bottle and the conclusion was that he might be having seizures. The added observation was that at times he was unresponsive and would stare, perhaps having a petite-mal$_{10}$ seizure. Our neurologist explained that not all children with irregular EEG's have epilepsy, even though all children with epilepsy have irregular EEG's. He told us to continue to observe this behavior and he would reexamine Danny on a regular basis to check his developmental progress. We continue to have a consultation on a yearly basis. Danny didn't have epilepsy and never suffered a seizure. This conclusion was only possible to make after a few years had passed. I now know that there are a significant number of children with Fragile X syndrome that do experience seizures, even though Danny was not one of them.

During this time, we did what parents must do in taking care of a sick baby. We tried to persevere, but it was harder because he was always screaming in hunger, then vomiting what he ate. Still, I fed him, rocked him, read and sang to him even though I felt there was little response. I was unable to comfort him and many days I waited for my husband to come home so I could escape into the hallway if only for a few minutes of quiet. I took an extended maternity leave to care for my baby. I also enrolled in a masters degree program, and arranged for a nurse to baby-sit for me. That only lasted for one short month. Danny was too sick to leave in anyone else's care. I could not possibly leave him and worry about him at the same time. Actually, I worried when I was there and when I wasn't, but I felt no one else would be able to respond to his desperate cries even though we also were unable to provide much relief. Many times, much to my irritation, I would awaken at night to worry some more, as if I was not worrying enough already during the day. I would worry about Danny's pain, his developmental delays, his survival, if I was personally doing enough to help, and his future.

We continued to have weekly doctor visits and Danny received shots of hemoglobin to assist in remedying his lack of nutrition and vitamin deficiencies. My poor baby was stuck with needles so many times that it was difficult to find veins to enter. He would scream the minute we entered the medical center. Later, when able to walk, he would lie down, scream and kick his feet to attempt not to enter the building. He correctly associated the building and doctors as a source of pain rather than an oasis of cure and lollypops as so many other babies did. It was the beginning of Mom doing what needed to be done even if that meant extreme discomfort for her baby. I felt the pain as well.

After his hospital stay at five months of age, we returned home and Danny began to gain weight. It was a slow process, but the pre-digested formula prescribed for him did begin to work. At seven months old, Danny began to scoot on his belly, however, he did not crawl until after he learned to walk. We just thought that Danny was one of a kind and was developing differently because of his lack of nutrition.

His great pleasure was his walker. It was the old fashioned plastic kind that unfortunately tipped easily, so it is no longer sold today. He was able to propel himself around on our carpet less floors without carpeting and used it as a great source of transportation. Our pediatrician felt that the more he was upright and moving, the easier it would be to digest his food. I knew this was farfetched. But it seemed to be working.

At three months of age, Danny was diagnosed with urinary infections. These infections reappeared as soon as he was off the prescribed medication. After repeated episodes, we were sent to a pediatric urologist in Chicago who decided after X-rays that Danny had a urinary reflux.[11] The remedy would be to leave him on medication until four years of age when he would outgrow this problem. We did not feel confident that this was the correct diagnosis, and later sought another opinion, but temporarily left him on medication.

We continually tried new foods and Danny was making some progress both health-wise and developmentally. We went through weeks of just rice cereal and formula and then introduced one food at a time. We wanted him to gain weight and thrive so we desperately battled his digestive problems. He was able to eat applesauce and baby food jars of meat and vegetables. We fed him propped up in a high chair. He was still unable to sit well without support.

Our pediatrician had very early diagnosed our baby as being hyperactive. His hyperactivity[12] was at this time typified by his continual kicking while in his sturdy wooden high chair. Danny was only still while asleep. At all other times his legs, arms, or both were moving, banging or waving. His hand flapping continued for many years. We were encouraged and hopeful, even though at seven months he was still vomiting. When diarrhea started it lasted at least two weeks. This was a continued problem that, although improved, lasted well into Danny's fifth year of life.

We lived in a suburban one-bedroom apartment until Danny was seven months old. At that time we purchased a townhouse and moved. He was seven months old and still cried all the time. We purchased from a kind couple that confided that their son had cried for nine months from colic and that was probably what Danny had. I knew by this time that it wasn't colic, but I didn't know what it was. Many strangers in stores and on the street also informed me that he must be hungry, or that I must be doing something to cause his crying. I wasn't, but I felt that I should be able to make it stop and I couldn't. I did worry, and although I knew that these strangers were well intentioned, it was depressing and discouraging to be unable to find a solution.

My husband Mike and I decided that if Danny survived his first year, we would make him a big party for his birthday. I cooked for a week and invited friends and family. We had a big dinner and cake. It was a miracle and we were grateful. The big shock came on the day of his party. Danny was leaning on my leg in a standing position and he ran across the room until he fell down. He couldn't crawl or get up after he fell. However, when we picked him up, he again ran, not walked, as fast as he could before falling again. Normal development included crawling before walking. Danny developed at his own speed, in his own order and we watched in delight. It was a long time afterwards, almost six months, before he learned to crawl, and then he only did it to get up to a standing position. He never walked around furniture or followed the normal developmental stages. We still had no idea of the root of Danny's developmental delays.

Following a schedule helped Danny adjust to the world surrounding him. Even after Danny physically improved, he still clung to his schedule of eating, sleeping, and playing. He woke very early, was fed breakfast, played in his walker, was given a bath, and after drinking a bottle, took a nap. This worked for Danny, but it took a long period of trial and error. All parents of special children must develop patience and consistency. Once the schedule is in place everything functions much better. I know that at times you as a parent will feel it is too difficult, but once the routine is established it will be well worth the months of work to make it happen. If the child knows what to expect, he or she will develop a sense of security. This is one of the most important feelings you can possibly give to help your special child. Keep to the schedule you determine works best and don't let shopping, eating or friends and family interrupt it.

After lunch we developed varied activities. At least once a week we traveled to the mall with a friend and her son. It is so important that as soon as your schedule is established to find a friend to commiserate with and also enjoy adult conversation with. The feeling of isolation for a parent of a special needs child can become very depressing and overwhelming if there is no one to talk to on a daily basis. I was fortunate since I had my husband, friends and family, in particular my parents. My Mom and Dad called me daily to check on Danny's progress.

If the weather permitted, I often went for a walk with Danny in his stroller. I added afternoon activities in addition to doctor visits to our schedule. Now Danny only needed monthly instead of weekly doctor appointments, so we were making progress.

At eighteen months, Danny was crawling and walking and delighted in these activities. However, his grunting was now beginning to become more noticeable to all around him. Our doctor again referred him to a Chicago hospital this time for a Laryngoscopy$_{13}$. He was put to sleep and a tube with a light was inserted down his throat to determine if there was an obstruction. He was diagnosed with loose vocal cords. This was a developmental problem that the Doctor believed in time would tighten and correct itself. They were right, but his physical and mental development continued to be a mystery. Danny was kept overnight for this procedure and we took advantage of the opportunity to request a second opinion for his continued urinary infections. The pediatric urologist determined his urinary reflux was a result of a valve on his bladder that wasn't functioning. He would need radio nuclide cystograms$_{14}$ every six months until the valve, he predicted, would begin to function on its own. The danger was that his urine could back up further and cause kidney damage; therefore, it had to be monitored carefully. He did not need the medication for urinary infections prescribed by the first doctor. It was another physical developmental delay. We learned to always ask for a second opinion and to trust our instincts when Danny was concerned. Danny was administered these radio nuclide cystograms on an out-patient basis until he was five years old, when the valve on his bladder did mysteriously began to function. That was a moment of enormous gratitude and excitement. I am constantly in awe of the human anatomy and amazed at how much development is taken for granted. I, for one, will never take anything for granted that is supposed to be automatic and part of the development from infancy to adulthood. I don't believe anything is automatic for a child with special needs. Everything must be taught, but the important part is to remember that it is possible for the child to learn it.

One interesting story was that Danny refused to drink his bottle at the hospital. We were using a bottle nurser that had plastic inserts to cut down on the amount of air swallowed during feeding. We tried everything to ensure less interference with his digestion. The hospital attempted to feed Danny with a regular bottle and he wouldn't respond. My husband went looking for Danny's nipples and nurser bottles at several pharmacies. He finally located them at a local drug store and returned with them. Danny then greedily drank the bottle. The nursing staff was amazed at the results and this is just another instance of parents understanding the needs of their child; it is similar to nursing infants not drinking from a bottle. When we first suggested this, the entire medical staff was in disbelief until they witnessed it first hand.

I cannot stress how important a routine is. Remember that it takes time and that it is different for every child, not just special needs infants. Try to feed, bathe, play, go for walks, and lay down for naps at the same time. Keep in mind that this is a matter of trial and error and listening to your instincts to find out what will work. Your infant will adjust better and you will find time to unwind if you stick to a schedule. Even hyperactive children will sleep as they approach one year of age if you are consistent. Try to put them down for the night before 9:00 to allow you a short adult time, and for a nap to allow a down time during the day. You might need that time for a nap, to complete housework, or to spend with other children. It will take time but consistency is the key to success.

Chapter Three:
Run Before You Walk.

Two of the key elements of Danny's development journey after reaching one year of age were to somehow catch up by learning to crawl, and to be able to pick up food and other objects. Since eating was his primary focus, we concentrated on this area. Everyday I placed interesting foods on his highchair tray and encouraged him to handle it. This continued for months with my lifting his tiny hands onto the food and assisting him to reach his mouth. We did the same thing with crawling but had little success. Mike and I would rock in all fours and crawl. Then we would hold Danny and attempt to assist him with crawling. In this way we tried to teach him to crawl. We didn't meet with any success, but we continued anyway. At least we felt that we were trying and we all enjoyed the exercise. This exercise usually ended with all of us laughing so hard we could hardly move. With feeding, it was different. First of all, he was very impatient, and second of all, he seemed to be confused and at times angry about my interference. When I finished feeding Danny I always left toys on his tray to encourage his using his hands. He would bat at the suctioned toy attached to the highchair but still not pick up anything.

Thanksgiving Day 1978 was the day Danny first picked up food in his fist and ate it. He was thirteen months old. We were delighted and everyone applauded. Now Danny had a grin from ear to ear! I had a table filled with food and a house full of people for the holiday, but the thing I remember most is my son starting to feed himself. This was indeed a monumental achievement. I always held his hands around his bottle when I fed him and it was this month that Danny also learned to hold his own bottle. I would place his bottle in his hands while he was lying on his back on his blanket, and although he was still unable to pick up the bottle on his own, he was able to hold it long enough to drink at least half of it's contents. I understand now that not only he didn't have the coordination needed for these activities, but he lacked the strength in his fingers to grasp tightly enough. He picked up toys as well as food with his fist and did not develop the use of his thumb and pointer finger to grasp until he was two years of age.

At this exciting time of accomplishments, Danny was totally unable to communicate verbally. When I look back at this time I remember our frustration as well as his with being unable to express his needs. He did not nod or shake his head to communicate yes or no. The only sounds he made were basically grunts. He would kind of hum in a deep growl when he chewed. I read to him and we always talked to him even though the response was minuscule. He did enjoy being silly and he enjoyed being tickled. His attention span was only a minute for whatever activity he had, so we were aware very early of his hyperactivity. Danny loved activity. He loved his riding toys and one in particular was a small horse that he could propel with his feet and move around. His attention was sustained to enjoy riding his rocking horse. This rocking motion of this activity continued to entertain him between eighteen months and four years of age. He also liked to watch and listen to his wind-up radio as we turned it. I found that removing his crib toy and placing it on his blanket allowed him to continue to look and play with it. Listening to music, especially with headphones, is an activity that he continued to enjoy as a teenager and today as an adult.

I enrolled Danny at "Gym and Swim" at the local YMCA, but he continually developed ear infections so we chose to only participate in the gym portion. We both enjoyed this change of routine and exercise. We also went to the mall with a friend and her baby on a weekly basis. Having a friend to talk to can be so important to your sanity. This gave me an adult to share conversations with, as well as allowing Danny an opportunity to sit in his stroller and observe his surroundings. I was also hopeful that by being exposed to a normal baby without special needs he might mimic other behaviors.

He would sit in his stroller for a long period of time if he had his security blanket. This blanket was actually a cloth diaper. Since Danny spit up so much, we always left one under him when he slept. Once he was able to grasp objects, although still with his fist, he carried it around with him thus forming an attachment. Now, he did us a favor picking this item to become attached to since we could have a number of them and could always have one washed and clean. Later, he specifically picked a fringed cloth diaper so it was more difficult to have duplicates. This was a source of security and a comfort to him that we were more than happy to see him develop. He never used a pacifier and didn't develop other attachments to blankets or stuffed animals until he was much older.

The other activity I enrolled Danny in when he was two was a musical program called "Come Children Sing." The teacher in charge was wonderful and allowed him to sit in the back to watch and listen for months before he was able to join in. He was shy and frightened at times, but after a short period of time he enjoyed participating. His favorite instrument were the sticks he could hit together. The program director later developed a component for special needs children, although Danny was too old at that time to participate. The instruments and singing were great fun and a great aid, I believe, for hyperactive as well as Fragile X infants. We registered for this program every week for two years. Afterwards we went to lunch at a fast food restaurant. Danny was now able to eat a plain hamburger.

Danny's diet continued to be one of trial and error. He was able to digest plain foods without milk products added. In addition, he could eat spaghetti and sauce, scrambled eggs, all beef hot dogs and bologna without fillers, anything with ground beef, and cooked fruits and vegetables. He ate a lot of applesauce, but juice (especially apple juice) gave him diarrhea. There didn't seem to be any reasonable explanation for his continued stomach distress. We were relieved on one hand, that Danny was becoming healthier each day. On the other hand, we continued to be perplexed as to his past and present developmental and physical delays. Most babies with severe allergies cannot tolerate tomato or egg products, but again, Danny was different. Danny was later diagnosed with an allergy, or intolerance to soy. That explained the difficult problem with formulas and the stomach distress when eating anything that contained soy.

Before two years of age, we took Danny to see a group of genetic specialists at a Chicago Hospital. He had already been tested for Fragile X a year before, and received his first false negative result. This group identified his characteristics of Fragile X but discounted their importance. I also discounted its importance and relevance. They measured his head and determined that it was smaller than normal, but concluded that other than that, they could not group Danny with any genetically-based diseases as yet recorded. They felt that his long face and large ears were hereditary and that was all. He did look like his father. The diagnosis was made that I was free to become pregnant without concern of passing on a hereditary disease since he did not have one. I do not look back at this with regret because I might not have had another child if I had known the correct diagnosis. I had no reason to doubt the accuracy of these findings.

We went ahead and planned to have another child. About a month before I delivered Bobby, I moved Danny out of his crib. He was already two and a half years old and although he loved his crib, since it gave him a sense of security, I convinced him that he was a big boy and should sleep in a big boy's bed. I made sure he was secure in his new bed before his baby brother came home and slept in his crib.

In May of 1980 Danny's brother was born. I was uneasy that Bobby could have some of the same problems as his brother. Every time he spit up I was worried. However, that worry was unfounded and he developed and reacted as a normal baby. Danny bent down and gave him a kiss that surprised all of us, and the fact that he wiped it off didn't even detract from the moment.

There was a stark difference between not only the physical and mental development, and also the physical contact with my new son. I was able to comfort my baby and fulfill his needs. It was at this time I concluded that Danny needed more help than I could give him. It was a combination of his lagging behind, not being potty trained, and not speaking that caused me to insist that something was wrong and enlist my school district for help. This was the beginning of my life-long job as my son's advocate. It was still unusual and uncommon to test children before they were three and very little was available unless your child was deaf or visually impaired. Most of the school districts had a wait-and-see approach to developmentally delayed children. We were fortunate that our school district belonged to a cooperative that administered testing.

At two and a half years of age we were ready to tackle the problem of Danny's hyperactivity. He suffered from attention deficit hyperactive disorder; now known as ADHD. Up until this point, I believed that we would be able to redirect his energies in a constructive manner through sports and other actives. Of course, I was in denial of the seriousness of the problem. I also began to face the fact that without medical intervention, Danny would never be able to concentrate and focus long enough to learn anything. We understood that medicine was available to stimulate the parts of the brain that controlled concentration. It was at this time that our neurologist and pediatrician suggested Ritalin$_{15}$. Our initial trial with this drug was a disaster. It seemed to help Danny to focus, but when it wore off late in the day he literally ran around in circles. I called our Doctor and he assured me that Danny would eventually tire and stop, but it was frightening to witness. We wanted to give up on medication, but his poor learning ability warranted another try. Up until this time he was unable to focus long enough to complete a simple puzzle. His normal reaction was to throw the pieces in frustration! We knew we had to help in some way even if that meant succumbing to pharmaceutical remedies. Our neurologist suggested the medication Cylert$_{16}$ and Danny still takes it today. No drug works for everyone, but without it, Danny would not be able to function as an independent adult today. I am glad we live in a world that has medical advances to assist us. I can't imagine life without it. Danny's hyperactivity has affected every aspect of his life, both then and now.

One day while at the shopping mall, Danny darted into an elevator. It was one of those afternoons when he was unable to sit in his stroller. As I ran to grab him, the elevator door quickly closed and my son disappeared from sight on his way down to the first floor. I was frantic, but we were spared from disaster when, after pushing the button for the elevator to return to my floor, the door opened and there stood my smiling Danny. He was oblivious to the danger and excited to have had an elevator adventure. Afterwards, I was even more diligent about never letting Danny out of my sight.

At this time, we were referred to an umbrella agency that covered several school districts including the one we resided in. That was the first time Danny was given a complete psychological test. At two and a half years old he now began to make a few sounds. Between then and three years of age he uttered single words or sounds. They included "Ma" "Da" and "Ba," but not much else.

I attempted potty training without any success, so that was delayed for almost another year. He was diagnosed by the school district as eligible for early childhood education beginning at three years of age. It was a "non-categorical"$_{17}$ program, which basically took in children with varying levels of developmental delays. He had a wonderful young, enthusiastic teacher who helped Danny a tremendous amount that year. He began speaking in two word sentences and playing with a ball. He received speech therapy and showed much growth. Danny stayed in that program for two years. It was situated in a rented single family home and was an ideal one-room schoolhouse type of setting.

The other children in Danny's class all lived in the same school district, even though the program was under the auspices of the umbrella-area special education director. When Danny was first enrolled, he backed away and made a whining sound when confronted with any new adult. He was bussed to school and although it was difficult to allow Danny to get on that school bus at three years of age, it was the best thing I could do for my son. He overcame his fear of his teachers that year and although he still did not play with the other children, he did watch and parallel play without complaint and sometimes much interest.

One of the strange parts of Danny's development was his fear of people. I knew from the beginning that it was not a form of shyness. He would become very anxious inside any store that was crowded. He would become hysterical at Christmastime inside a mall or store that was filled with people. The circus field trip from school was disastrous. He became uncontrollably shaken. We never took him to see a movie because once the lights were out, even if it were not crowded, he would begin to scream. He wasn't frightened of the dark at home but couldn't handle it elsewhere. There was no magic solution for this occurrence. He just grew out of it, but it took many years. He was not comfortable watching a movie until he was seven years old. I became very careful about taking him to places that were unfamiliar and crowded.

We now understand that Danny was exhibiting "tactile defensiveness,"[18] but at the time we didn't have a clue what it was called or even that it existed. This is a hypersensitivity to touch as well as an avoidance of touch. This explained our frustration in not being able to sooth our crying infant by hugging, holding and touching. In addition, he suffered from "hyper-arousal."[19] This caused him to pay too much attention to what others are able to tune out. He was further frustrated by "hypo-arousal"[20] that prevented him from receiving information. He often did not respond to important messages. This included his not responded to verbal cues and directions, as well as

21

visual ones. These simple terms and explanations were not available to me at the time and I was left attempting to understand what my son was feeling when he couldn't and didn't react as other children did to their environments.

Potty training was a long and arduous ordeal that went on and on and on. At least, I felt that way and worried about not seeing an end in sight. At two and a half we didn't have any success so we waited until he was three to try again. I tried training pants to help him feel the wetness. But that was unsuccessful and very nerve wracking to me since the accidents were all over the house. Then, I tried placing him on the potty after breakfast since that was when he seemed to regularly have a bowel movement. At three and a half years of age that seemed to work. I never put training pants on him when leaving the house until he had mastered using the bathroom at home. He was four years old when he was finally trained. I considered the accidents just that-accidents. The unfortunate thing, in addition to his trying to regulate his body, was the uncontrollable diarrhea he sometimes had. He experienced accidents for many years and we always sent a change of clothes with him to school. We sent that change with him in case of emergency until he was in high school. Thankfully, by that time it only happened once or twice a year. His stomach problems and frequent diarrhea exasperated the training, and I knew that he would not become fully trained until he was more in tune with his body.

Another hurdle I had to assist Danny with was to learn to dress himself. Every day for a year we worked and tortured each other attempting to teach Danny to at least partly dress himself. He did not have a cross-over ability₂₁ and therefore couldn't work his right hand on his left side of his body, and again this was a dilemma we weren't fully aware of at the time. Every day, I laid his pants in front of him and verbally gave him clues as how to put one pant leg on at a time and then to pull and tug the pants to pull them up as he stood up. To another parent, these everyday workouts would seem insane and some days I thought, they were, too. I can't tell you what day he finally succeeded in this task, but I can tell you that it was the better part of the year until he was able to put on his own pants. I felt that this hurdle had to be crossed to enable Danny to become fully toilet trained. Otherwise, I reasoned, he would be dependent on telling whoever he was with to assist him at all times whenever he needed to go to the bathroom. This would make becoming toilet trained at school virtually impossible since he barely was able to identify the need to use the bathroom until the second before he had to be there. Sensory integration is a contributing factor that delays toilet training success. Many Fragile X children are not aware of the need to use the toilet until the moment before because they are not very well attuned to their body messages. Add that to the communication delay and now we have only seconds to spare before an accident occurs.

I learned that Danny could be taught but patience and time were necessary to reach success. Some days, both were in short supply before the school bus came. When Danny mastered any life skill he then would complete it faster than anyone else and still does. He could beat the firemen going down the poles when he gets dressed today.

One of the first times I was forced to be Danny's school advocate was during the second year in his non-categorical preschool program. He was seen by a speech therapist and she was insistent on teaching Danny sign language. She felt that he would drop the signs as soon as he discovered that speech was easier. The problem I had with that philosophy was that speech was very difficult for him and it might never become easier. Also, Danny was making fast progress in his speech and communications skills. I was afraid of doing anything that would impede that progress. I consulted with his pediatrician and with his nod of approval, refused sign language instruction. This was the first time I had to speak on behalf of my child's best interests but certainly not the last time. I agreed that we would entertain the suggestion again if in a year his speech progress did not continue. We never had another speech therapist mention the need for signing.

Between the ages of three and five, Danny developed preservation-type speech patterns where he repeated words over and over. This is a characteristic of Fragile X children that we were totally unaware of at the time. We were happy that Danny was developing speech and not very concerned with that abnormality.

During the summer of 1981, we decided to take our first real family vacation and travel to the Wisconsin Dells. We packed and left with enthusiasm. We stayed in a small one-story motel in the heart of the excitement. The first afternoon we went to an outdoor amusement park filled with enchantment and rides for children. Before dinner, Danny was coughing a little, but did not seem to be sick. In fact, he wasn't sneezing or developing a fever. I wasn't too concerned until he began to wheeze. Months before, he had a cold and had been diagnosed with asthma. The symptoms disappeared as soon as he was well. I recognized the cough and bought an over-the-counter medication. Late that night, he became worse and was passing out. I knew we needed to get to a hospital as soon as possible. We didn't even know where it was and there was no phone in the motel room. No one answered at the office so I flagged down a passing patrol car and after refusing an ambulance, grabbed Danny for a police escorted drive to the hospital. This was the first of many asthma attacks, and we endured countless adrenaline shots[22] until new methods of treatment were found.

A year later, Danny was seen by an allergist who explained that we should not wait for an asthma attack, but instead should treat it preventively. His asthma would occur without warning, and at least for the time being, we were told he could not be cured. In fact, Danny never outgrew his asthma but learned to treat it so he could enjoy and live a normal life. He uses inhalers twice daily and we have a machine called a Nebulizer[23] at home to give breathing treatments as needed.

One problem that Danny had was taking medication without upsetting his stomach. Once diarrhea began, it would last for weeks and cause pain as well as accidents. We discovered that it was the syrup in the medication that caused these bouts of distress. Once we found a decongestant in pill form we witnessed an immediate improvement in his stomach distress as well as his overall health. First of all, the ear infections that he had with increased frequency ended, and secondly and equally important his breathing improved.

The second part of Danny's treatment centered on allergy shots. We had him tested with a skin sensitivity patch test. The only surprise was that Danny was highly allergic to soy. That explained his distress in digesting baby formula based on soy products. Other than that, Danny's entire back swelled. He was basically allergic to everything. He started taking allergy shots soon after that and continued for more than five years. He was almost 13 years old when he stopped.

He knows that preventing breathing problems can only occur when he is in touch with his body. This again was a learning situation that took many years of trial and error of treatment in the hope that Danny would learn to recognize the symptoms before they were too severe for us to treat at home. The wheezing was easy for me to identify and that was the telltale sign when he was younger. The problem worsened when he reached puberty and basically stopped breathing instead of wheezing. He needed to recognize the danger before his airways closed. For whatever reason at that time Danny began to feel the difference when his chest tightened and alert us. I am sure it was being in touch with his body at this time that enabled him to survive through many breathing crises and not fall victim to a fatal asthma attack.

Chapter Four:
Television is Not Your Enemy

In order to fully explain the need to watch television, I must take you back to the earliest recollection of its use with Danny. At six months of age, Danny was still spending the majority of his waking hours in varying amounts of distress for various reasons. He wanted to eat and was experiencing hunger. He was frustrated at not being fed fast enough. He was in pain caused by urinary dysfunction, or was having stomach pain. All of these unfortunate occurrences caused Danny to scream, cry and complain. I tried to comfort him in every humanly available way. He wouldn't take a pacifier, and he didn't respond to rocking, or holding and walking with him. There were many days when I repeatedly tried each and every way to comfort my baby. After all, I reasoned, every mother should be able to provide that comfort.

Feeding Danny at this time continued to be an all day ordeal and a frustrating one at that. Almost every time he ate, he vomited most of his food intake and then experienced hunger shortly afterwards. This resulted in a lot of crying, whining, and a very unhappy baby. At this time, I would have understandably tried and continued with anything that gave him relief even if it only was short-lived. The swing was helpful in the very early morning, but not in the afternoon. This daily routine of misery continued even after we found a formula that he was able to digest. A very gradual daily improvement was made, though, and improvement was most apparent when Danny began to walk at one year old.

One afternoon when I was at my wits end and Danny was about six months old, in desperation for some distraction, I turned on the TV. This was unusual for me. I had promised myself that when I went on maternity leave, I would never become the type of woman to stay home and vegetate in front of the TV to watch soap operas. I stayed true to my vow, but that day I discovered something new. Danny stopped crying and watched the television. He especially liked the slow moving dramas with laughter sequences. He would sit in his infant seat and become mesmerized by the screen. I was amazed and relieved that I had discovered something to make Danny actually laugh instead of cry!

Over the first year of Danny's life, he became very attached to Mr. Rogers. I feel it was the slow and kind manner that he spoke with that enabled Danny to understand, react, listen to, and above all, pay attention to him. Somehow, his hyperactivity slowed and his attention span increased when Mr. Rogers was on television. Danny continued to watch him happily for many years. It always amazed me that a child that couldn't sit or focus on much of anything was calmed by television. It relaxed him, and at the same time, allowed him to focus and concentrate. At times he did zone out, but even that seemed to be a way for him to achieve quiet time.

I am not suggesting that you should plan to sit your special child, or any child for that matter, in front of the television all day long. It is, I feel, one of the many resources available in the 21st century that can be used to benefit your child. I am also saying that you should not feel guilty or hesitate to use what works to calm and nurture your child.

At this time, we were unable to take Danny to the theater to see a movie. He was afraid of the crowds, and he couldn't be expected to sit for two hours. He couldn't even sit for 20 minutes. So the alternative was to watch videos and movies on television at home where he could move around freely. He loved watching fairy tales and could watch them over and over again identifying all the characters, as well as gaining an understanding of good versus evil. He particularly loved Batman and his antics with Robin. He developed a special relationship with these characters, which later led to his collecting their comic books and dressing like them on Halloween. It also gave him many hours of play with the action figures. This all was a result of watching television. It certainly increased his imagination and thinking skills.

Even as an adult, he enjoys reruns and can watch his favorite movies dozens of times. Today he is able to go to the movie theater but continues to delight in watching television and movies at home. Growing up, his favorite toys were his radio and his television and they still are!

Danny began by age two to look at books and listen to stories of his favorite fairy tales that he also watched on television. We had to hold on to Danny to restrain his running and movement as we read him a bedtime story each and every night. However, we never had to restrain him to watch television. It was an activity that held his attention.

The other interesting development was that Danny loved baseball. At two he could throw but not catch a ball. It was at this age he began to watch baseball on television. I am not sure how this occurred because, although I enjoy live baseball games, I never watch it on television and neither does my husband. There was something about this game that struck a chord with him and it is not something I can explain. I can tell you that Fragile X children have their likes and dislikes, the same as other children. Although I can't predict success with many toys or books I can tell you that television watching is not evil and can be effective as an activity. It was and still is an age appropriate activity that he still loves today as an adult.

As Danny grew, so did his insistence in viewing television. He would watch it whenever he could. The minute he came home from school or today comes home from work, he watches various programs. It is an activity that still helps him relax. That word relax is crucial for special children and adults. Without it, they would be prevented from living an independent and productive life. Maybe something else can be found to do this for your special child, relative or patient but this is what worked for Danny.

Television and radio continue to be Danny's connection to the world. He watches and listens to the news daily and is able to communicate all current events that happen in his community, city, and the world. He follows the politician's speeches, and with assistance, votes at the polling place alongside his family. He is unable to read the newspaper and depends on broadcast media to inform him on world events. Although he does sometimes tire of the news and switch to a movie, he does this as a decision-making adult. He is indeed lucky that so many choices for keeping informed are available today. I am grateful that he is able to understand the complicated world we live in and that television has been a comfort as well as an ingredient for intellectual development for my son.

I feel that, as with any activity, choice is important and if the choice of activities involves television, it can add to your special needs child's life and development in a positive way. There is not one simple answer to correct all communication needs, but television is one avenue to be explored.

Chapter Five:
School Days

Danny attended a cross-categorical kindergarten in a typical school setting that he was bussed to. He didn't have the luxury of attending our neighboring school, and that was not objectionable to us since we didn't feel our district could meet his needs. We were again blessed with a wonderful, experienced teacher that delighted the children with her enthusiasm. The lesson that I learned from her was in the form of advice. She noticed that I worried, worked with, and continued to try to teach Danny as much as I could, even though much of the time it frustrated both of us. One day when we met in the neighborhood in which we both resided, she told me something I never forgot. This wise teacher told me to not continue to be Danny's teacher, but instead to give myself permission to enjoy being his mother. As a teacher, I had not even considered that I needed to be a parent first, and not concentrate on the teaching role I had been trained for. This was a deliberate decision I made that day, and I feel it improved my mother-son relationship.

I was driven to attempt to eradicate his delays and remove the possibility of his not being able to learn as other children did. Danny would learn at his own speed and there was nothing I could do to change that. The fact that he was learning was encouraging, and I felt let off the hook at this point for accepting total responsibility for his progress.

I still worked with him, but not continually. I never gave up being his advocate and that is one message all parents of special children must be prepared for. No one can or will be able to guide your child to success better that you as a parent. Some administrators, teachers, and other professionals are terrific and some are not. You must always be there for your child but not necessarily teach them yourself.

After a year in this two-year program, Danny was sent to a communications delay classroom. He was bussed with some of the other children from our home district to another school. This was Danny's primary diagnosis and it seemed to be the right one. It was, however, during this year that we determined otherwise. First of all, he did not begin to read or write during that time and when observing the classroom I discovered that his teacher rarely talked. She used so few words I wondered how she was modeling speech for the children. In fact, when I mentioned this to a supervisor she also observed the classroom

31

and agreed with this amazing occurrence of lack of speech by the communications teacher! This is another consideration for parents of special children. Always, always, without exception, visit the classroom before agreeing to place your child in it. The classroom atmosphere, setting, and interaction with staff, as well as between children, is of the utmost importance and can easily be observed without any difficulty when class is in session. It is your right to observe and if the school balks at the idea you will know immediately that a problem exists.

Now that we determined the school program was inappropriate, we then had to find one that met his needs. This was difficult because I did not want to admit to Danny's development being delayed, let alone accepting the fact that Danny might, in fact, be mentally retarded. It was a pivotal time for me. Did I need to accept who Danny was in order to help him overcome as many obstacles as possible? When I was able to answer that question I crossed the threshold of denial and opened the door to the pathway of success for our son.

I took Danny to a Chicago hospital to be tested to determine with an impartial professional psychologist the degree of his disability. It was important to me that the best testing be completed away from the school district to give me a better understanding of his abilities. No one mentioned Fragile X Syndrome as a possibility. The Intelligence quotient testing was inconclusive. He was borderline between learning disabled and mentally retarded with a 71 I.Q. This is, in fact, higher than he tests today and I believe that the numbers are somehow higher at a younger age but decrease due to the lack of development later. I really have no other explanation. Keep in mind I am writing this book and reflecting on Danny's life experiences from a parental, not a physician's perspective.

I visited numerous classes with the school cooperative's supervisor, and found that Danny would fit best in the developmentally delayed classroom that was labeled MMI for minimal mental impairment. He continued to receive speech and occupational therapy and continued to make progress. The question I repeatedly asked myself was, "Is my son retarded?" This was a difficult time for me, but I was more determined to find solutions and assistance for Danny than I was concerned about his label. I had to find the best educational setting to meet his needs and I was driven then and for many years afterward to achieve that end. Whatever means were necessary to help Danny would be worthwhile.

The teacher guided the children and used positive reinforcement. She had her students use play money to pay for numerous rewards, and I again witnessed Danny learning. At this time he was very resistant to my instructing him at home, so I felt less effective. I felt that since I was a teacher, I should be able to teach my own child how to read. However, he had difficulty tracking and it continued to be a very frustrating activity. In addition to his tracking problem and his hyperactivity, he experienced reversals. This reversal difficulty continued through adolescence. It was so severe that when asked to repeat or even identify a letter he was unable to determine the difference even when they were both present. So, add to the equation a child that could not differentiate between letters d, b, or p, q, as well as letters m, n and sometimes c and o, you can understand the dilemma of learning to read. Danny never learned to read easily, but he does manage by learning sight words. He was never able to develop reading ability by phonics, either. This underlines the importance of trying different approaches. Not all children learn in the same way and with Fragile X children, phonetic instruction, although popular, may not be the answer.

Socialization was and continues to be a dilemma for Danny. We believe that even if Danny were not Fragile X, he would prefer to be a loner. His pervasive lack of relatedness at times causes him to withdraw into his own world and become unable to relate to others. We have always fought this character trait in every way we possibly could. When he was an infant I took him to the YMCA, to "Come Children Sing," joined a parent-infant playgroup, and exposed him to other children at the park and our local swimming pool. In other words, I was able to create social situations even if he only watched and parallel played instead of participating. As he grew older it was more difficult. After all, it is acceptable to push an infant in a swing, carry him in the pool, and have him watch others as a toddler but as an adolescent it was odd and unnerving for others. I involved him in as many activities as I could that were socially age-appropriate. It was easy to accomplish this until he was five years old. It was at this age that I needed to identify some other social avenue.

It was at this time that I registered Danny in our local Special Recreation Association. I cannot adequately portray the wonderful experiences and social development that this organization provides all children and adults with varying disabilities. The first experience Danny had was with a summer softball team. Belonging to this team offered him an opportunity to experience fun, physical activity and learn in a non-threatening environment. We were thrilled. We were very lucky that our local park district joined this association. It is not something that would have occurred to us at that time as a viable solution to provide Danny with social activities if it had not already been in place. After that experience we have continued to enroll Danny in any and every activity that interests him. This continues to offer him recreation as an adult that otherwise would not be available to him. It is part of the continued push for equality for the citizens with disabilities living in our communities and one that all parents should avail themselves of.

Danny continued to be bussed to different schools in different communities. Many times he was bussed with the same children from previous special education classes. We never complained as we felt a need to continue his education in the best possible way to benefit Danny. With my husband at my side, we attended every parent-conference and annual review. Meetings were difficult for us since we always listened as details of Danny's learning difficulties were outlined. It is not that they intended to be negative; I just found the news depressing. As I look back, I know that somehow I always waited for the news that he was catching up to other children his age. Part of the reason for this delusion was that no one was able to diagnose Danny as having Fragile X syndrome, and therefore we didn't hear any diagnosis as to his ability levels or potential. We again had Danny tested for Fragile X, but received a false negative result.

One of Danny's friends in his school had a birthday party and Danny was invited. Keep in mind I use the word "friend" loosely since the mother just asked for a class list to invite others for her son's birthday. What I saw that day was my first encounter with a child diagnosed as Fragile X. When I came to pick Danny up the birthday boy was sitting in front of the television in a rocking position. He was oblivious to the others around him. The excitement and confusion

34

of the birthday activities were obviously too much for him and he overloaded. His only way to deal with the sensory overload was to zone out into his own world. I now know that many Fragile X children have autistic characteristics. Danny did not display the rocking, but the hand flapping and, at times, the trance-like behavior was a constant component of his behavior. As he developed and as time passed he was able to control the hand flapping, and now only does it for very minute times when at a sporting event or watching one on T.V.

The birthday boy's mother confided in me her guilt for passing on this terrible hereditary disease. I remarked to my husband that evening that I didn't know how I would react if it were me. I already carried enough self-doubt about not being able to change Danny's abilities and really did not think I needed to add another burden. Of course, I also didn't believe that Danny had Fragile X. After all, the test results said he didn't and I had no reason to doubt the test's reliability. I continued to search for answers for my son. Today the Internet enables all parents to locate information at the tip of their fingers but in the 70's and early 80's no such help existed. Some days I am in tears when I contemplate how Danny's life would have been different if he had been born 20 years later. Of course, then I also conclude that I might have not pushed as hard if I had known. Would he have developed into such an independent man? This is a question that I cannot answer. Somehow, through his journey of development, he has become a success, even though that success was filled with many days of anxiety and anguish for my husband and myself.

Danny continued to be bussed to different locations that had space available. He received school services including speech and occupational therapy. Speech therapists were plentiful but occupational therapists were not. There was a limited availability of occupational therapists for a number of reasons. First of all many educators felt the services unnecessary. They were convinced and tried to convince us of the ability of the classroom teachers to provide these services. Secondly, they could make a substantially greater salary in hospital settings, and thirdly they had to travel from school to school. Today it has been widely accepted and documented that occupational therapy is a necessary component for Fragile X children's development, but in the 80s, no such information was available. Occupational therapy was necessary to enable Danny to overcome his sensory integration difficulty. Somehow I witnessed the improvement Danny made with occupational therapy and fought to continue it without any specific understanding of the physical and medical reasons and rationale.

When I say that I fought for these services I am referring to the yearly IEP$_{24}$ meetings where we listened to the experts tell us that Danny no longer was eligible for occupational therapy. I was even told by one therapist that Danny should have O.T. services provided by his classroom teacher. She further stated that only the more severely physically handicapped children should be seen for occupational therapy. I was basically told that even though Danny needed help he wasn't delayed enough to receive it! I continued the fight for Danny to receive these services until he reached seventh grade and received O.T. on a consultant basis. This was one of the first times I experienced the need to say I know what my son needs and I will agree to nothing less. Since I refused to sign off on the discontinuation of services, the school district continued to provide this assistance. The message here is that parents do know what is best for their child. I did, and I did not have the luxury of having experts to back me. That has changed today and this can assist you in your journey.

My first description of the crossover phenomenon was by an occupational therapist. She explained the necessity of its development and why Danny needed to work both sides of his body with his right and left hands. It was information to which we had no other access. This therapy assisted Danny in snapping and improving strength in his fingers to enable him to fasten his pants. How independent could you be if you are unable to snap your own pants closed? A whole world of improvement opened its door when he received these services. I wondered why anyone would suggest discontinuing them. Of course, we know that school districts, no matter how well meaning, still have to balance their books. Occupational therapists often draw an hourly salary and become an easy target to eliminate. Many self help skills as well as fine motor skills were learned directly from occupational therapists. Danny could learn but he had to be taught. One of the skills that many teachers felt was not worth the effort was learning to tie his shoes. He learned after many years of wearing Velcro shoes. Now, of course he does it the easy way. He just leaves them tied and slips them on and off! However, if it comes untied at work, he doesn't have to ask someone to tie his shoe since he is able to do it himself. For an adult, not being able to tie your own shoes could cause enormous embarrassment. I felt that he really needed this skill and even if it took much longer it was one that he needed to master. This is just another example of an everyday activity that has value in the quest to becoming an independently functioning adult.

Chapter Six:
Back to Work

In 1984 we were living in a two-bedroom townhouse and I was contemplating returning to work. Danny was seven years old and his brother Bob was four. I knew that aside from needing the extra income, I now had to consider the fact that my extended maternity leave was over. If I wanted to return to teaching I had to return that spring. I waited as long as I could, since I knew how much I was needed at home, and also that I had devoted and felt compelled to continue to devote as much of my day as possible to assisting Danny in all he attempted to accomplish. I reasoned that he was in school all day, and I would only need to leave him with a babysitter for an hour in the morning and a half hour in the afternoon. I was ready to make the change from stay-at-home Mom to a working Mom, and with the help of our wonderful neighbor, Danny was too.

The first week I returned to work was a disaster. My babysitter's son came down with a case of chicken pox. I did not know how sick Danny would become if infected with this childhood disease, so I could not risk the exposure. My family saved me by taking turns babysitting for the first two weeks. Dad, Grandpa and my sister-in-law each stayed with my sons until the other children were no longer contagious. The irony was that within two weeks, Danny developed chicken pox anyway! Both Danny and his brother had a full-blown case that lasted for six weeks between the two boys.

Our neighbor, who also babysat for us, cared for the boys during this childhood illness since she was assured her children couldn't catch it again through my boy's exposure. I must add that we were so lucky that this wonderful friend agreed to baby-sit. She was and is an angel in disguise. I never had a moment of worry. She cared for my children as if they were her own and was wonderful to Danny. He still remembers the many happy days he spent playing at her house. No one ridiculed him in any way. Total acceptance is a rare commodity and one that we all treasured and appreciated. Still she went beyond that and loved each child that she encountered. They played outdoors as much as possible, where Danny rode his hot wheels bike and played ball. He was with others and watched as they interacted. It often was not something that he was able to participate in but was as much social interaction that he was capable of.

We encountered a significant problem the next year. Bobby began kindergarten with a sweet, old-time kindergarten teacher. The school was not at all academically oriented and that was not going to meet his needs. He began reading at the age of four and there was no program to accommodate a kindergarten child with those abilities. They were doing worksheets that he had mastered in preschool. We had to move in order to meet Bobby's needs and we also needed to remain in the same area so the cooperative district would feed Danny into the same school and program where he was currently a student. The dilemma was to attempt a move to improve Bobby's education and still not disturb Danny's placement.

We found a great house that we still live in today. It is in a community where everyone walks to school, rides their bikes in the street, plays baseball and joins the Boy Scouts. This was perfect for Bobby and enabled him to attend an academically challenging school. Not everything worked out as smoothly for Danny. We now had the challenge of finding a new babysitter for both boys. I was desperate and asked everyone I met. We were again lucky that first year because we located an in-house day care that would take both boys. It worked well since Bobby could walk there after his half day of kindergarten and Danny only needed to be there for short spans of time. Danny wasn't difficult to supervise because he was happy to watch television while waiting for his bus in the morning or for us to pick him up in the in the afternoon, and his brother was there to assist him if the need arose.

The next few years we managed to always find neighbors willing to assist us in caring for our sons while we were at school. When one after the other returned to work and we were eventually unable to find a new one, Bobby was old enough to have a key. He was always very responsible for his age and we believe that was because of Danny. For some reason, we were unable to understand why he felt responsible to help his brother from a very early age. It was never a role we chose for him but one that he chose for himself. By third grade Bobby was in a gifted program and it was enlightening to have the two extremes in one household. Learning was as easy for Bobby as it was difficult for Danny.

Danny had attended five different schools by the time he was in fifth grade. Now even though we felt he was receiving a quality education, all of these moves were difficult for a child that thrived on schedules and routine. The cooperative located its' classrooms in whatever district school volunteered and had the extra space. If enrollment increased, they would have to change locations the following year. When Danny was in fifth grade, they wanted to locate him in a suburb that was an hour drive from our home. The hour did not take into account the time involved and needed for pickups and drop off at each house for the other students. That would have meant at least an hour and a half ride each way and we couldn't and wouldn't allow that. There was a law in effect even then, that stated children were not supposed to be bussed further than an hour from their home. That was the year when I became acquainted with the district superintendent of our elementary district.

I called our superintendent's office numerous times. I reminded him that we were taxpayers too, with children whose needs were not being met. I begged him to intercede on the special classroom's behalf and to find some space somewhere in the area for them. I offered (or threatened, whichever way you want to look at it) to speak at the next board of education meeting. Actually, I requested that he put me on the agenda for the next meeting. What I did not know at the time was that our district superintendent did care. You see, he also had a special child. When I detailed our dilemma and I had the nerve to ask him to clean out a storage room and convert it to a classroom, he was really listening. That summer before school began, he had convinced a local school district to take this class for a year and the following year our home district allowed a special education classroom to be located in our school! Danny could now walk to school with the other children in the neighborhood. We thought we were in heaven! It was a remarkable gain that so many other parents of non-disabled children take for granted. This was the first time Danny would attend school with his brother and walk to school with other children. No amount of money could possibly pay for this priceless experience. His teacher was transferred with her classroom and now Danny finally had what others in our community took for granted.

Bobby was not accustomed to having Danny there and since he was very protective of him, he also had to learn to adjust. Bobby's fourth grade teacher reminded him that Danny was able to function before coming to his school without his brother, so he needed to give him some space. He also needed to trust his teacher, staff and Danny himself to handle whatever was necessary. This was a hard pill for Bobby to swallow, but somehow he did adjust to allowing Danny to coexist in the same school. Bobby was able to still look out for Danny without pestering his teacher to check on him daily.

It was a transformation that took place many times over the years they attended the same school. Danny and Bobby didn't exhibit any sibling rivalry or fight at all until much later. I think that it might also have been a delayed developmental stage and one that wasn't fun to witness when the boys were in high school. It's a good thing that I didn't know that it was delayed so I didn't know what misery lay ahead when I had to witness Danny not getting along with his best friend Bobby. As Danny matured, he realized that his little brother should not be allowed to shoulder all the responsibility or ever tell him what to do, and he let his brother know in many rude ways. Even though Danny was less able, he did develop a talent to insult and irritate the one person who cared for him the most, his brother. It gave him a sense of power and it took Bobby many years to understand this unfortunate behavior.

Our neighborhood adjusted very well to having their first special education class housed in our school. Many or most of the school population, including teachers, had never been exposed to children with less than average intelligence. The first complaint I heard was from a parent during baseball practice that had remarked how horrible it was that "retarded children" were coming to our school. Another parent responded that she thought it was wonderful to allow this class to coexist here. The other parent was a special education teacher and although I was delighted to hear her response, I had concerns about the silent majorities reaction. My fears were unfounded. Almost everyone at the school was terrific including the principal. He would ask Danny to raise his arms when he saw him in the hallway and then tickle him! Danny loved the attention. Of course, the principal only did this because he was Bobby's brother. After the first giggle, the principal and Danny formed a great relationship.

There were a few unfortunate instances, but I attribute these to individual personality problems that occur to all children. One difficult situation occurred when the gym teacher told me that since Danny did not talk to him, he would not talk to him either. That was a problem of a poor attitude and not one that I could change. It was the last time that we had the problem, but not the last time the teacher did. The problem was with him and not with Danny. Discrimination against the handicapped can be outlawed, but you cannot make people be nice or change their personality. That is a useful piece of information for all parents. I always requested a parent-teacher conference when there was a problem. This school was always ready to meet to discuss and attempt a solution. I know that not everyone is that lucky, whether your child is in special education or not.

Before we moved to this new home, Danny was an active participant in the local Special Recreation Association. When we moved we were dismayed to find out that our suburb was not a member. Danny had a desperate need for this social outlet and I was determined that he be allowed to continue to participate in it.

As it turned out, the association was attempting to enroll our suburb and after speaking with the association director, I agreed to attend a meeting of our local parks and recreation department. At that meeting I spoke to the board to request funding to gain membership and enable special children as well as adults to enjoy the benefits of recreation. They were very receptive and after hearing from some other parents and future participants they voted to approve the money. I was amazed and delighted. Danny participated and enjoyed and continues to enjoy many different and exciting social programs and events including how to ride a bike, swimming lessons, softball, social club and training for the Special Olympics.

At five years of age, Danny wanted to learn to ride a two-wheel bicycle. We took the training wheels off his bike because he leaned so heavily on them that they bent. We devoted many hours to this activity and he just was not ready. It was one of those times when determination was not enough. Still, every spring, we would take Danny out and either my husband or I would run next to him to assist his balance and bike riding. We enrolled him in "Learn to Ride a Bike" from Special Recreation for three years. Countless volunteers and staff continued the lessons until he finally achieved success. He eventually learned to ride his two-wheeler. Once Danny masters a skill he continues to practice it effortlessly. At eight years of age, Danny could ride faster than his mother and father could. I was so happy that we did not give up even though it took much longer than anyone else would believe. We felt it was worth every minute of the time.

After Danny mastered riding his bike, we encouraged him to ride his bike around the block after school. One day, my neighbor called and asked if I knew where Danny was. I responded that he was out riding his bike. She then informed me, to my horror, that he was directing traffic on the corner. That put an end to his unsupervised bike rides and we reconsidered his maturity. He still was not capable of making safe decisions. He continued to be very impulsive, doing whatever he felt like and not considering the repercussions.

As Danny reached the age of twelve his brother was in band and needed to leave the house earlier in the morning to attend practice. It was difficult to find a babysitter because now Danny was bigger and no one was willing to baby-sit for a preteen. Our neighbor's daughter agreed to walk him to school and again we were saved from quitting a job. We could never leave him alone and we refused to ask Bobby for any sacrificing of his activities. It was at this time we registered for Respite care$_{25}$. We were dependent on this service for all emergencies, half school days and for that rare night out that my husband and I would treasure. This agency not only took care of Danny but also would watch Bobby too, at no cost to us. It had a waiting list of over a year but when we reached the top we availed ourselves of this wonderful service for a ten-year period until Danny was able to care for himself. Like everything else in Danny's life, that day was worth waiting for. When it came, I was amazed at how long it took to reach it and how quickly the time had gone.

Respite care is available throughout the United States and although the requirements for membership vary, most will assist parents of special needs children and many times of adults. Danny needed a health care professional because of his severe asthma attacks for a span of a few years and after that, many of the respite care workers were full-and-part time special education teachers. Our experience with this agency was wonderful. The caregivers were caring, devoted and responsible individuals that came into our lives at a critical time.

We were able to find male babysitters for my sons until the babysitters reached the age of about sixteen. Then I was unable to employ a preteen girl and could not locate a boy older than Danny. At the age of eleven it was virtually impossible to find a babysitter. When Danny was tiny no one seemed to object to his being different but as an adolescent and later a teen many other same-aged adolescents and teens were frightened of him. In addition, when I searched the neighborhood for an early morning babysitter I found that adults reacted the same way and no one was willing to have this special needs child in their home. This in not something that anyone could do anything about, but it did cause us to pause and reassess his future. Once you became acquainted with Danny, you would lose this fear, so we learned to only approach residents that were personally aware of Danny through his brother and that seemed to work. You can understand the need for respite care when faced with this dilemma.

Danny always had crooked teeth, but in the scheme of things, we were not too worried. Still, we took him to an orthodontist for a consultation. They assured us he was in need of braces to correct not only his crooked teeth, but also his crooked bite. We were told if he did not have this corrected later, he would experience jaw problems later. Now, I have not mentioned the fact that for some unknown reason Danny cannot open his mouth very far and definitely cannot hold it open. In addition, Danny has a severe gag reflex. This was a dilemma for his regular dentist, but a very difficult problem when braces were concerned. The orthodontist assured me he would devise an apparatus to hold Danny's mouth open. He used a thick rounded plastic stick that he inserted across the back of Danny's mouth to hold it open without causing him to gag. This worked and he accomplished a beautiful job straightening his teeth. I was working at this time and I was suddenly, after a few visits, informed they would only give me an appointment first thing in the morning. I was shocked that I was asked to take all those days off of work when they not only had afternoon but Saturday hours as well. I later learned that the reason for this was the orthodontist wrote, "extra time needed for this patient-do not use regular schedule" across his chart. He only allowed them to schedule Danny in the morning, and did not want him on Saturday since they had shorter hours then. Basically, he was sorry he had agreed to accept this handicapped patient. This was one of my first experiences with discrimination, but not my last. I personally called the orthodontist to attempt a compromise and he finally gave in to giving me Saturday appointments, but told me that I should not expect special treatment. I reminded him that seeing my son was not special but equal treatment. I realized that time was money to him and that since Danny took more time, he regretted seeing him. Ironically, all the doctors and nurses from this orthodontist office loved him and still inquire about him.

At the same time Danny was experiencing frustration at school because his progress had slowed. He was unable to read at higher than a second grade level and did not complete work assignments independently. This meant that his worksheets not completed at school were being sent home to finish for homework. We tried, but if the student is already frustrated and tired when he arrives home, then homework should not be expected to succeed. In Danny's case it resulted in tantrums and total misery for his mom and dad. My husband and I tried taking turns with Danny. We tried alternating afternoons, and we even tried doing half of it for him. None of this seemed to avail us of the misery we all felt. This frustration did not accomplish anything and at our next parent-teacher conference we discussed the problem. It was the teachers point of view that Danny could accomplish what he needed to at school and that they would try harder to sit with him to accomplish this end. He was becoming increasingly unhappy with his lack of ability, even though he was unable to express it. I was still not able to teach him to read, but not wanting to leave any stone unturned, we asked if the school's regular education reading teacher could tutor him.

This reading specialist took small groups of children that were experiencing difficulty in reading for additional help. Danny was grouped with much younger children, but the teacher had him assist her with many tasks such as passing out books. He enjoyed this daily class. Did he learn to read? No, unfortunately, he did not but at least it was another avenue that we explored and one that did not cause additional anxiety. He just was unable to gain the skills necessary for

reading, writing and math progress. This does not mean that he did not gain at all. The slow gains simply did not move him as quickly as he needed to go to be ready for high school.

This was also the time when we gave up attempting to teach Danny cursive writing. Many teachers had attempted this feat with almost no success. For some reason, Danny was only able to print and even that was a struggle. His fine motor skills never fully developed and we had to just help him move on with a shrug. We rationalized that many doctors also had poor handwriting skills and so Danny would survive with whatever scribble he could muster. He continues to verbalize "sorry about my poor handwriting" when asked in the work world to write something, and that seems to work for him. As long as he could print his name on the back of his check that was all he absolutely had to do. We have always assisted him with job applications and other necessary forms and continue to do so into adulthood.

For seventh and eighth grade Danny was mainstreamed for homeroom, music, gym, and for social studies. He is an oral learner and was, therefore, able to understand and gain much information during these classes. All the teachers that had the opportunity to have Danny involved in their mainstreamed classes loved him. This was a new experience for Danny and he thrived with their attention, even though most of the time he was a silent observer and not an active participant. His classroom special education teacher always assured us that Danny would be a success even if he never read a book. Her confidence in him is something we will always treasure. He is the one student that she will remember as hyperactive, kind, and able to achieve in the real world. Her dedication is an inspiration to all parents, students, and administrators that are lucky enough to come into contact with her.

We are a Jewish family, and we would have sent Danny to Hebrew School if he had been able. He had enough trouble learning to speak in English to prevent us from ever considering introducing him to a second language. We did, however, send Danny along with his brother every Sunday to Sunday school. We spoke to the principal and teachers beforehand to enable them to prepare and familiarize themselves with other students with disabilities. They were more than willing to incorporate their lessons for one more student even if that student lacked the abilities of the other students. I was delighted with the opportunity to mainstream Danny in this way. He rarely participated fully but certainly was made to feel part of the class and welcomed to join in the activities. It definitely was non-threatening.

After reaching the age of fourteen, we decided to attempt to have Danny tutored to become Bar Mitzvah. Age 13 is the normal and expected time to be called to the Torah and to participate in a Sabbath service, and that is the time when it is believed that all Jewish children reach adulthood. We had delayed this celebration for a year and now we felt it appropriate and able to attempt it on a small scale.

We shortened the service to an hour and changed the day from Saturday to Sunday in order to be able to arrange a private service. Danny was shy enough in front of his family and would not have been able to cope with others in the audience. We wanted to have as little anxiety as possible for this occasion, and still allow Danny to participate to his fullest ability.

He attended private tutoring sessions weekly to prepare him for this service. His tutor stood next to him during the ceremony and prompted him when needed. It was a beautiful and meaningful morning for Danny and all in attendance. Afterwards, we celebrated with a brunch at a local hotel. That was a happy time for Danny and one of many memories that we will always treasure. We were delighted that we were able to successfully lead Danny through this normal and challenging activity.

This was also the year Danny graduated from elementary school and left everyone and everything that was familiar and comfortable to him behind. His homeroom teacher presented him with a framed classroom picture and his music teacher with a mug that he still treasures today. That picture is displayed prominently on his desk. Danny walked down the aisle proud of his accomplishments and unfazed as to the challenges that lay before him. He was aware that he was leaving his favorite school, but he was unaware of where his next step would lead him. He left that worry to his family, and it was a gigantic worry. When looking back, I must acknowledge that this was one of the most difficult times I had to endure to enable Danny to secure his hold on future success.

Chapter Seven:
Graduation and High School Choices

The next dilemma we faced was crossing the bridge from elementary school to high school without the wonderful support system that enabled Danny to thrive. His graduation was within sight and I was unaware of the tremendous turmoil that we as a family were going to face. It began when I visited our local high school during Danny's year in eighth grade. I observed the special education class Danny was scheduled to enroll in the following year.

The high school itself was wonderful. It was filled with bright energetic students in multi-colored hallways. The administration was friendly, and after making an appointment, I was ready to observe Danny's future school. Nothing prepared me for the horror that existed within those classroom walls.

Upon entering the classroom, I was greeted rudely by some of the students and observed the anxious teacher at the front of the classroom attempting to teach a current events lesson. During this instruction, two students were lying on their desks without any attempt to move. Three other students were engaging in name-calling and angry discussion. While this was occurring, the teacher called on a student to answer a question and another student called him "dummy" when he was unable to answer correctly. Neither the teacher nor the teacher aid attempted to involve the sleeping students, nor was there any intervention to resolve the disruptive and aggressively behaved students. The teacher acted helpless and discouraged, but certainly not surprised by their behavior. I observed for two hours hoping that as time went on the classroom decorum would improve. I waited to speak to the, by now, exhausted teacher after class to inquire about other options. I asked numerous questions and did not receive any encouraging or satisfactory answers.

I inquired about the withdrawn students and the ones I observed not having the ability to respond to answers correctly. I was determined to find some answers for questions that were really too disturbing even to verbalize. However, I was there and so I did ask. I wanted to know, in particular, how he would teach the students who could not read the material he assigned and the worksheets passed out to every student. He explained that his teacher aid would assist and attempt to read the assignment orally to the nonreaders when time allowed. He added that, basically, everyone was taught at the same level. Now, my disappointment turned to horror.

I determined that this was a mixed-ability grouped classroom with totally cross-categorized disabilities. Some of the students were diagnosed as behavior disorder; others were learning disabled as well as some with the minimal mental impairment and attention deficits that my son was diagnosed with.

I was discouraged, and at the same time, frightened that my son would have no choice but to join the ranks of this awful classroom. What could I do? I had come to observe, never once believing or imagining that this classroom would not become Danny's for the next four years. If it was to become his high school, I knew that his education would end and he would vegetate in a withdrawn, head-down position for the duration. It was a terrifying situation and as I contemplated the effects on his future I concluded that my new mission in life would be to save my son from this classroom prison, locate someone to help, and find some other school setting to fit his needs. This school was not going to fit the bill.

Time was at a premium. I had less than six months to find a high school for Danny. He might be a broken toy as his little brother had referred to him so many years before, but I was determined for him to have a productive life filled with experiences that would enable him to be independent and not rely on others to constantly repair his dysfunction. I could not allow this school setting to curtail his progress and prevent him from blossoming into a functioning individual. The question that stymied me was: How would I accomplish this monumental feat?

The first method I used was to call on every contact that knew Danny to develop a support system and sounding board. I needed constant feedback and encouragement from both personal and professional individuals. I already had a strong personal and family support system that had enabled me to travel the difficult road to success and allowed Danny to become the young man we saw in front of us. My husband, son Bob, parents, family, and friends were there for me on a daily basis to encourage me and to remind me of the important task on hand. Danny had me and me alone as his sole advocate. I knew his future success literally depended on my success. It then did become my mission in life and a daily trial filled with many setbacks.

I began the journey by personally contacting the supervisor of special education for our district. He gave me the expected speech. He felt the program was more than adequate to meet Danny's needs and could be adjusted to meet his IEP objectives. After clearly disagreeing with their assessment, I thanked them for their time and then continued to search for others that could possibly be of help in my desperate journey.

Each day, I went to work and came home to make phone calls. This was a time before cell phones, so I did not have the access that we have today. In a way, it was better that my day was not interrupted, but rather separated by this dilemma. I could not make calls at work or the car so many times I had to leave messages for calls to be returned to me the following day. This method seemed to work, since it was usually the case that my calls were not returned, allowing me to inform the secretary of this and request that the individual be called to the phone. Most of the time, I was calling schools that employed personnel working past the student dismissal time and was able to initiate a conversation at that time.

I wanted to network with every supervisor and teacher in our metropolitan vicinity to gain information and contacts with successful programs. I knew that many supervisors and administrators would be hesitant to speak candidly and that I would experience greater success with teachers since they were more likely to describe their programs accurately and honestly. If only I would have had the Internet access available today, I would have been able to locate everyone with one email! I also could have located many advocates to hire and help me in my quest. Alas, I did not know of the vast technology of the future, so I used all that was at my minimal disposal.

I had one person that assisted me and that would have been a surprise to all. It was our districts' elementary school psychologist. She spoke with me weekly and never ended the conversation without a suggestion. Her support was priceless and I don't know if she ever realized how much of an asset she was.

I spoke with directors that, after describing their program and hearing of Danny's disabilities, added that they couldn't meet his needs either. There were very few programs in place that considered job training and job placement an integral part of their program. I became convinced that a community-based program was the answer to Danny's school placement. It was a new and exciting type of program that considered the whole person and their abilities rather than their

52

disabilities. Now that I found the program and the location, how would I convince my district to place Danny there? It was not in our neighborhood school and would require expensive bus service.

I never knew that I had the strength to remain so resolute, determined and transfixed in finding a satisfactory high school placement. I never gave up the fight because I was focused on Danny's future. I cleaned closets while awaiting phone calls to burn off tremendous nervous energy. I also spent many sleepless nights planning my next move.

I called school board members but achieved little success in that direction. Upon reflection, years later, I believe it depends on the political inclination of those on the board. I know that currently I would have more success with that strategy, both because of the makeup of the board and my experiences requesting assistance. The more active you become, the better chance of success you achieve, mainly through continued practice of negotiation. Some board members take a greater hands-on approach to the academic structure and functioning of their schools, and would therefore be more able to make adjustments for special needs students. The push that was popular at the time, was to place every student in his or her neighborhood school. This is the focus that affected Danny's placement. This placement was a delight in elementary school and allowed for Danny to attend our elementary school that was within walking distance. This only was successful because of the program and the fact that his special education teacher was terrific. It allowed him to not only walk to school but also receive the best education. Now he was being offered the walk to a neighborhood high school minus the education!

One obstacle I faced was the short amount of time I had to perform this miracle of finding Danny an acceptable high school. Danny's annual review and IEP meeting was scheduled for the first week in April and as the time approached I was not even close to a resolution of the problem. My next strategy was to request a delay of this meeting until June. Now, of course, this made all involved unhappy since they wanted to end this conflict by finishing the staffing and having me sign for high school placement. I did have the right to request a rescheduled date to enable me to attend and that is just what I did. Since the psychologist from our elementary school was one of my silent partners, she just rescheduled and coerced the other participants to somehow agree to the delayed meeting.

This was a stroke of luck for me. It gave me time to visit programs and inquire about services available. I questioned the student to adult ratio and the communication skill development. I also met the first professional advocate it was my pleasure to encounter. She offered me free advice and a phone number to reach her privately. She performed this service for a fee for others and I was delighted to meet her. I did not even know that such a service existed. Remember this was 1989 and changes and rights were new for the handicapped. Much has changed and the Internet had not developed to the current stage of access.

At the same time, I repeatedly called our high school district superintendent. I began low key by detailing Danny's life story. His reply was to tell me he would investigate and get back to me. Instead he called the district's special education supervisor to intervene for him. Remember, that is the first person I had called many months before with no success. When I received his phone call I was very discouraged. He was angry that I had talked to his supervisor and attempted to convince me to end my objections and take what our school district was able to provide financially. The fact that it did not meet Danny's needs was of no concern to him. I informed him that I could not and would not agree to placement in that classroom. He was not happy with me and at that point, as much as it was unsettling to not have reached a solution, his anger was not something I was able to resolve.

I was running out of time and energy. I called our District Superintendent one more time. I again reiterated my exasperation with not placing Danny in our local high school. I went so far as to ask him what he would do if it were his child. I knew I had one last desperate plea and I had to make it work. It was then that I said, "I do not want to go due process, but I will do whatever it takes to provide my son with a fair and equal education." Somehow that was all it took. He agreed to send Danny to any high school we felt would meet his needs and bus him there. The same special education supervisor that was at this time and point feeling quite resentful of me had to make the arrangements. The ironic part of this story is that we spoke many times in years to come and he did change his angry disposition toward me. He later respected my desire to only do the best for my child and told me so. It was a long journey to reach that point, but a miraculous one at that. The sense of relief was indescribable and sweet. I must add that Danny was totally unaware of the time and frustration I encountered in order to ensure his smooth transition to high school.

During this time of Danny's development, we were contemplating adding a pet to our immediate family. I was overwhelmed with work, going to school to attain a Master's degree, and attempting to continue to be Danny's advocate. I felt completely devoid of extra time and energy. My husband and both boys were focused on adopting a dog. I felt that I had delayed my goal of attending school one night a week for as long as I was able and had somehow inserted it into my already busy schedule. In order to fulfill that goal, I knew that it would take years of dedication and a family willing to fill in for me while I was in class. Mike fed and cared for the children during my absence and both boys enjoyed the evening when Dad "cooked" fast food. When they wanted to visit the pound I reminded them that Mom could not and would not feed, pet, train, or pet this dog, and they promised that it would be their responsibility. My family was already showing their responsible side by successfully taking over household chores, so I felt I would reconsider their desire for a dog. I never had a dog growing up, so for me this was something I had never thought of as a necessity. Mike was the one who felt all boys benefit from the companionship and ownership of a pet. They promised to be totally responsible for the dog. Danny pledged to be more responsible for himself as well, and that was quite a challenge for me to refuse.

One Sunday we visited the shelter and requested a Shih Tzu. It is one of very few dogs that do not shed and are suggested for asthmatic children. The volunteers were surprised and asked how we knew there was such a dog in their possession. We, of course, did not know, but somehow I suppose it was meant to be. Danny took one look at the dog and it was love at first sight. He took the leash and walked the dog around the building. We were astonished at the immediate bond.

That afternoon, we took a family vote. With three votes for and only myself abstaining, we agreed to take the dog home. She was very well trained, and the bond with Danny continued to amaze us. She did not affect his allergies and the only other surprise was that I fell in love with her too. Danny was and continued to be as responsible as he promised to be the day we brought the dog home.

After that, any difficulty we had with Danny acting responsibly was easily corrected by reminding him of the dog agreement. The first thing Danny does when coming home from work is to let the dog out into our fenced back yard. We never have to remind him to fill her bowl or to give her a treat. He was a great friend to our first dog, Annie, and continues to be for our second dog as well. He considers her his best friend. The moral is to attempt pet adoption for your special needs child. Again, it might not be right for all children but you will not know unless you try. Our dogs have had a positive and significant affect on Danny's developmental process.

Chapter Eight:
High School and Transition

Each and every change is difficult for Danny, however his transition to high school was smooth and not very stressful. It was then that I knew I had made the right choice for him. He was anxious the first few days since he did not know anyone that attended this school. No one else from his previous schools was there. Those students were all attending their neighborhood school. To Danny's amazement, though, after a week, he discovered two other friends he knew from special recreation were in attendance but in a different classroom.

This school curriculum was focused on educating each student by using the community's resources. They incorporated every lesson whether it was math, writing, or spelling into their life experiences. Daily schedules were made and followed. For the students unable to read, pictures were used. They understood students' need for order and structure and these weekly schedules helped to organize their life.

The days were filled with plans to shop, cook, count money, and use their skills to complete these tasks. Everything revolved around applying for and completing a job.

Danny's first job was to fill pop cans in the lunchroom. This skill involved sorting, focusing, planning, verbalizing, and physically performing the task on a daily basis. Each morning students both with physical and mental handicaps would group together with a teacher and congregate in the lunchroom. They would then discuss what the task involved and how they would accomplish it. The actual filling of the pop machines followed this discussion. Everyone can identify with the frustration of placing money in a vending machine expecting a cola to be returned for money inserted, only to be greeted by a grape soda instead. Once the students understood this they were more than happy to fill the machines in the correct order since the student population of teenagers depended on them. Danny loved his first job and could barely contain himself to wait for his turn to fill the machines. During this period he did still exhibit some hand waving and that was difficult for him to control in this circumstance when patience was needed. His first job gave him the much-needed confidence to succeed in his future endeavors,

The remainder of his day was spent writing his schedule, planning outings, and reading what he wrote. When he went out into the community he wrote a grocery list and learned to pay for the items himself. Handling money is of the utmost importance and he learned the "dollar over" method. Using this method he counted out the dollars he needed and then added one more for the change. Danny was unable to count back change and the philosophy of this method allows the disabled adult to function in a money transaction without worry of much loss of money. After all, how many adults also neglect to count their change? Using only singles is an added key element to this program. It worked very well, although Danny was shy about contact with store employees as well as with anyone new to him. This continues to be a dilemma for him today as an adult.

His speech teacher worked with him on communication skills. She had him practice introductions needed in daily interactions. They spoke in groups and with partners. They went out for breakfast and ordered their own food as well as paid for it themselves. Nothing they practiced was separated from the curriculum, but rather an integral part of it. This was how the community-based program worked and experienced success.

Danny went to the mall, bowling, and to play video games. Everything was planned for age-appropriate activities. When they went to the mall together they were allowed to buy candy, anything else they wanted, or to just hang out. This enabled them to do the things other teens were able to be involved with easily, without parental supervision. Besides, what high school teen wants to go to the mall with their parents? They were excited and motivated to participate as each student was an active participant in the program. Danny was able to shop and complete activities that he otherwise would have passed onto another adult to complete for him. This encouraged his independence and ability to function in the real world and not only within the confines of a classroom. This reinforced my belief that the community-based programs were the most successful educational approaches. I do not believe that enough schools utilize this approach, and I only discovered this wonderful program through much research.

An important component of this program was the communication skills taught by the speech therapist. Danny had speech three times a week, but participated in communication practice on a daily basis. One of the skills addressed was use of the telephone. In order for Danny to stay by himself, even on a very limited basis, using the telephone was a necessity. He needed to be able to call for help and speak clearly enough to explain what his problem was. Danny was always hesitant to use the phone. Truthfully, although he does answer the phone now as an adult, he never got over his phone phobia. One of the techniques his speech therapist used was having Danny go to a pay phone and call her at her desk on a regular basis. She awaited his phone call and it became a little easier each time he attempted it. We had no concern about his communicating with friends in this way, but rather our concern was for Danny to be able to use the telephone if he needed to. As I mentioned previously he does answer the phone when it rings but will only talk briefly. I often wonder how differently he would react if he were not FragileX. Would he still experience the shyness that prevents him from completing many tasks in his world, or would he have overcome that shyness? These are questions, I am afraid, are without answers.

One skill that Danny was able to accomplish at school with practice was reading charts and graphs. This activity is extremely handy for reading the television guide schedules and sports reports. He is able to follow his team names and to determine who won and by how many points. He can then announce what is on television for the day or night. Since these are his favorite forms of entertainment, they hold much significance to him. It also allows him to read the orders at work. It became an important life skill.

One significant part of his high school's program involved mainstreaming. They mainstreamed their special education students as much as their abilities would allow. From the very first week Danny was part of the lunch crowd and learned to stand in line, order his food and pay for it. There were different lines for different food items so there was always an aid to assist and assure that all the students ate. At this time of his life, Danny enjoyed the excitement and activity of the regular education students that would entertain him as he ate. It was not a frightening place for him even though it was crowded. He had overcome his anxiety of being in crowded places. I do not know exactly when this occurred, but it was a welcome change for him as well as for his family. This meant that we could now travel to amusement parks without worry of Danny becoming frantic.

He was mainstreamed for physical education all four years of high school. He was not always able to participate in each activity or accomplish physical feats but he did attempt to the best of his ability to participate. This attempt was appreciated and respected throughout his high school career. He was known throughout his school for his smile and agreeability. His coordination did not allow for jumping jacks or basketball to look like they should and this was tough for him. He did not want to practice even though we have a basketball hoop in front of our house. As it turned out with his current height of 6' 1" he would have been a star, but the desire and coordination were not present. Baseball was another story. He loved to play even though he was not able to hit the ball. After many years of playing on a special recreation team and constantly striking out he gave that up. He continues to love to watch the sport of baseball on television and at live games. He attended every Little League and high school game his brother played in. He was a wonderful fan and was even allowed to participate as a batboy for one season.

An ironic situation occurred during his junior year in gym class when one class accepted him too much. Someone treated him just like the other students and placed one of his shoes in a different locker as a joke. The teachers were livid and severely reprimanded the entire class reminding them to treat others with disabilities equally. Danny laughed afterwards since he realized he had not been treated differently but like one of the guys!

Danny was also mainstreamed for home economics and general science. Each year a different subject was attempted for mainstreaming. He always enjoyed it and attended with a teacher aid. Some of the material was read to him and tests were given orally. He is an oral learner and this enabled him to remember much that was taught.

His reading ability did not improve during his high school years except that he developed a better sight vocabulary. This sight vocabulary was the basis for his functioning in the real world. He was able to remember significant words and recall them if he needed to. He attempted some computer skills and writing as well.

During his sophomore year, he worked at the local library. These jobs were a part of his curriculum and a job coach worked with each student, the teacher aid on site, and the community to ensure a smooth transition. For this job, he sorted cards and stamped books for checkout. It was not enough action and involved too much stillness to make Danny happy.

His next job was at the county court house. He enjoyed that because this job had more movement and activity. The job basically involved running errands within the building.

His first school-based job that led to actual paid employment was at a pizza restaurant. He set up and filled the salad bar and also prepared the pizza dough in the kitchen. When their workday ended, they were paid by allowing them to make and eat their own pizza. This restaurant hired Danny, who was now sixteen, to work for them for minimum wage during the summer. He felt a new sense of accomplishment and worked there until a new manager arrived. The new manager was not attuned to assisting the handicapped and only would hire Danny to wash dishes at night. That was the end of Danny's first job. We were far from discouraged. It was a wonderful beginning and we felt that it held promise for his future employment.

Danny's job coach placed him at a motel next. This job was composed of cleaning and making beds, basically a maid's job. Not only did Danny not like the job, he was unable to continue it due to his asthma. Some of the cleaning caused breathing problems and he could not work at a job that adversely affected his health. He was not disappointed since he did not like the job, anyway.

He loved his next job opportunity. He learned to bus tables at a small restaurant. They allowed him to eat anything he wanted for lunch as payment and that delighted him. They bought him a cake to think him on his last day but not one waitress offered him a tip the entire time he cleared their tables. This seemed mean to us, but Danny enjoyed the work and never minded not receiving a paycheck. It was another valuable work experience.

The job-training program was geared to the student's interests, and depended on the ability of the staff to convince employers to hire the handicapped. The request was for employment without pay for a training period, and then to hire at minimum wage afterwards. There were some employers that paid the students after a two-week training period, some that paid immediately, and others that only offered job training. Any agreement the staff was able to make with future employers was a win-win situation for both the students and the businesses. This opened the door for many students to develop independence and job experience in numerous sites. Some of the students were trained in food service and others in janitorial as well as retail business.

One of the most interesting classes Danny was mainstreamed in was drivers education. Now we knew that Danny was way too impulsive to ever have us contemplate allowing him to drive, but the classroom driver's education was fun as well as educational. He knows the rules of the road and never hesitates to remind us not to speed, and in general follow all the rules. He was an active participant in all simulations except the actual driving experience. On one hand, it was a hard pill to swallow for him not to be allowed to drive like his brother. On the other hand, he told us he would crash too many cars and would never consider actually getting behind the wheel. That was one time he was able to acknowlege his shortcomings without admitting he was disabled. Somehow, whenever that type of conversation occurred he would reply, "I don't want to hear about it." This included any conversation about Fragile X. He is better able to deal with the knowledge of his disabilities without any labels and we have allowed him to have his wish. He knows there are many jobs and activities he is unable to accomplish that are age appropriate, and yet many that he can accomplish. We continually remind him of his many abilities and accentuate the positive to build his self- esteem. This plan of high expectations continues into adulthood, and I feel has met with great success.

During Danny's senior year he was given a tutor. This girl was earning volunteer points from the National Honor Society and was a wonderful asset to Danny's education. She was accepting and he was thrilled by the attention. This is another program that improved Danny's communication and outlook of the world. He listened to the news and watched many news programs so he had a broad range of age appropriate interests and knowledge to share with others. He paid attention to this volunteer and would have tried any classroom suggestion she made. All schools should make an attempt to provide mentors in this way. Communication within and without the special community is vital.

We had no way of knowing that the next job placement would result in a job for life. He was placed at a fast food restaurant and continues to work there today. He never had a job coach on site since they have a policy of training their own employees. The job coach did, however, remain in constant communication with the managerial staff and with Danny to ensure a smooth transition for him to become an independent employee. It was vital that he not only complete the job tasks, but also to communicate with the managerial staff and other employees. This fast food employer welcomed Danny with open arms and encouraged his participation in every activity that he was capable of performing. He became their french fry chef and also performed many other services needed for customer service. He began working mornings three times a week during the school day for a total of nine hours. He gradually increased his working hours during the week and later added Saturday for a total of between twelve and fifteen hours per week.

One of the problems Danny had to overcome was his lack of endurance. On one hand, he had hyperactive energy and on the other he had difficulty channeling this energy to remain focused on the task at hand. This caused him to tire easily and it was one of the mysteries of his life as to how he overcame these disabilities. I believe it came with maturity and a desire to succeed at a job he loved. Many times it took a hundred percent of his strength to focus and concentrate and thus causing him to tire after short periods of time. He was able to snack and that also helped him refocus. He could have anything he wanted to drink but the other employees always cautioned and teased him about caffeine. He definitely did not need any! Danny has a great sense of humor and that endeared him to his fellow employees. He loved to joke with them and they quickly accepted him. His skill levels and communication skills improved because of the wonderful group of people he had the luck and privilege of working with. I cannot thank them enough.

During Danny's high school years, transportation was provided to all work sites. We drove him to and from work on Saturday, but we were aware that a future problem would involve transportation to work during the week. My husband and I are both teachers with a long commute and could not drive Danny in the morning. The dilemma we would encounter was since Danny did not have the stamina to work a full day, we would need to locate transportation to work for him. He worked close to his high school and a twenty-minute ride from our house, unless we were traveling in rush hour. We would not be able to take him to work. One solution was to find another job that was closer to our house.

During Danny's senior year while others were planning jobs, college and advanced training we were again faced with making plans and decisions for Danny's future. What to do to continue after a great four years of high school is critical for our special population's future. If learning does not stop for regular education students, then it also must continue for special education students as well. If not, are we determining that they can no longer learn after becoming eighteen years of age? This is a ridiculous idea but one that is still currently practiced. The push is for placement in workshops[27] and group homes[28] at this age. I feel that it is too early to make that kind of commitment. If it is the conventional wisdom to continue education for others until twenty-one years of age then we should also continue education for our special education population. I am a proponent of some type of transition program[29] to assist in placement and continued education.

Danny graduated after his senior year and at the annual review we discussed the fact that although he would attend the graduation he would not receive his diploma until after he completed the transition program. Graduation was an exciting time for Danny. He was sad to leave his high school, but some of his classmates would also attend the two-year transition program. He remembers that day when he marched down the aisle and threw his cap into the air with the rest of the graduating seniors. He received balloons and celebrated his accomplishment with his friends and family with a giant smile on his face, and amazingly, without any hand flapping.

Danny's high school transition program started the following autumn. The plan was to keep his current fast food job as well as find another job closer to home. In addition, he would endeavor to improve his reading and writing skills and continue progress in becoming an independent adult. This would become a reality through continued community involvement.

It was near the end of his high school career that he learned to lock and unlock the door. He also began to care for himself sufficiently, allowing us to leave him alone for short periods of time. Until then, we had left him either with his brother or with a respite care worker. We began with very short periods of time and gradually increased the time frames to a few hours during the day. It was much later that we were able to leave him alone during the evening. We again tried leaving for very short spans of time after dinner, and slowly increased it. We left a spare set of keys with a trusted neighbor and always checked his bag to insure he carried his inhaler as well as his keys with him before he left the house. He was now arriving home before us in the afternoon and became responsible in doing so. He had the skills necessary to let himself into the house, and care for himself as well. That included getting a snack, and letting our dog out into the back yard.

Danny had, at this time, also become more attuned to his body functioning. His health improved, enormously since he was now able to use preventive rather than corrective medicine for his asthma. In the past, I was forced to listen for breathing difficulties and guess at distress. He developed the ability to warn us of chest pain and shortness of breath as well as headaches. This is a behavior normally identified by the age of three to five in normally developing toddlers. Since Danny was out of touch with his body, and he had a very high threshold of pain, he did not notify us until the moment before catastrophe. For example, his severe sinus headaches had resulted in vomiting and a full day of recovery. Once he could verbalize the pain before it became severe, a simple pain medication prevented the side affects and usually cleared the headache in less than an hour. His asthma was, of course, much more serious. He needed to be reminded to use his inhalers twice a day to prevent attacks. When he became more aware of the onset he was, with some training, able to use his inhaler to also prevent a more serious attack. This became a vital part of his independent life skills enabling him to care for himself even if only for short periods of time. When he experiences an asthmatic episode, we add the medicine to his nebulizer, allowing Danny to turn it on and use it when needed. This is all part of our son's life, filled with grasps for survival and independence.

It is inconceivable that our knowledge of Fragile X syndrome at this stage of Dan's development was almost nonexistent. As time passes, and doctors and hospitals complete so much testing as a matter of course, it is difficult to realize so little of this testing existed only a few years before. After all, we had Dan tested twice for Fragile X and the results were negative, causing us no reason to question the results. During a routine check-up, our neurologist described the advanced DNA testing for Fragile X syndrome now available and explained the discovery of many false negatives resulting from the tests used in the past.

In May of 1991, the CGG expansion$_{30}$ was identified and the FMR1 Gene$_{31}$ was named. This led to the current DNA testing. We were astonished at the realization, but also unwilling at first to succumb to more testing. My first question was: Is there a cure? My second question was: To what benefit would there be to know? We have never been the type of family to bury our heads in the sand. However, we had raised Dan without this knowledge. How could we benefit by a new diagnosis?

I left the Neurologist without agreeing for further testing. Somehow, I knew that Dan must undergo this next, but probably not the last test, to attain some answers for questions we had for many years grieved over. Still, this was one time I resisted agreeing for at least a year. I am still amazed that it took me so long to agree to find an answer. I had searched for a diagnosis since Dan was born twenty-one years before, and continually anguished over the lack of explanation for his condition.

The blood test was a simple one that came back with the shocking revelation that, in fact, Dan had Fragile X syndrome. Although I always wondered what the cause of Dan's developmental delay was, the results now confirmed the answers. It was with amazement that upon searching the Internet I now could identify the reasons and possible roadmaps for education and life skills for people like Danny. Why couldn't this have been available to me earlier? If I had known would it have made life easier? Would I have done anything differently? I now had to ponder those and many other questions.

I never blamed myself as many Fragile X syndrome parents do. After all, I had no way of predicting to whom this hereditary disease could be passed, since I did not know of any cases in my family history. I never was tested for this disease and neither was anyone else in my family except for Bob, my younger son. We left that decision for him to make. We explained that he could choose to take the test then or wait until he was older to determine if he was a carrier. Since Bob had been determined at an early age to be gifted there was no worry that he also had the disease. I now know that many times this disease does strike more that one sibling, so we were relieved that when Bob succumbed to the testing, the results showed he was not a carrier, and therefore, did not have to be concerned with passing this disease to his children. As far as we know, no one else has Fragile X syndrome in our family and that is a relief as well as a question that remains unanswered as to how it was transmitted. Maybe one day, I, will take the blood test to acknowlegde I am a carrier. I know that we somehow managed to raise a young man able to function in today's world without any scientific knowledge to assist in the journey. Children born with Fragile X syndrome have it easier today with many organizations available to them. One day I believe a cure will save families from traveling the journey that Dan has traveled.

Chapter Nine:
Transition and Beyond

Honestly and unfortunately, our high expectations for Danny's two-year high school transition program were not met. The program was disorganized and poorly run. It was separated from the high school and located in store front rooms that were part of a strip mall. The philosophy was that these students needed to disassociate themselves from their previous high school life. The school program was primarily composed of the same small group of ten students Danny had graduated with, in addition to ten students that had entered the program the previous year. The problem occurred, when the staff was not supervised, and lacked the experience to develop a successful program. We felt that Danny was better in the program than without it. We always attempted to suggest improvements, and to not let Danny know of our disappointment. He loved the days he was able to work and was bored the remaining days. His unhappiness demanded our investigation and questioning as to the appropriate program placement and his continuing in it. During the days, he stayed at the transition "office" he played video games, cooked, went to the library and laundromat, and unfortunately, just sat around. For my son, the answer was that he was ready for the work world and unhappy with the school setting. He was transported by van to work three days a week and then four days when a second job was found after six months. The school not only took and picked him up from his fast food job, but also located a busing job at a restaurant close to our house.

For Danny's second job, transportation was to be a new adventure. We had to petition for a handicapped card to enable Danny to use the special bus service provided for the elderly and disabled in our community. We were shocked at the tremendous amount of paperwork and red tape involved in this process. First of all, we had to prove that Danny was disabled. Now you would think this was a simple case of providing neurological documentation, but it was not. For some reason, they questioned his need for this service and insisted upon further proof. We were assigned an agency to investigate, and after communication with the counselor, I finally invited him to attend the annual review scheduled for that month. He was embarrassed and extremely uncomfortable as he sat and listened to Danny's latest psychological evaluation and IQ. He commented meekly that we would receive the bus pass in the mail, adding he had no idea why he was asked to investigate Danny's obvious needs. Transportation is, and continues to be, one of the obstacles preventing handicapped adults from achieving employment. Being unable to drive and depending on bus service impedes many able adults from adequately earning income. As we discovered, even the first step (which was getting the transportation pass) was made next to impossible unless you had an advocate working for you.

We received the bus pass and we were able to arrange transportation to the local restaurant three mornings a week. On those days, Danny would be transported by bus to and from our house. He attended the transition program for the remaining days and they transported him to his other job at the fast food restaurant one day and one day he stayed in the school. We took him to work on Saturday and so now Danny was working five days a week. This was a great accomplishment for him to achieve and we were proud of his work. When he began to complain about attending the one-day at the transition program, we knew that Danny now had achieved a sense of comfort and success in the real work world.

The second job location was great, allowing him to travel, work and return home independently. Our suburb subsidized the transit system, enabling Danny to travel inexpensively. He worked at a nice, clean restaurant requiring him to wear a white shirt and dress pants. The only problem was the many difficulties we encountered difficulties with the managerial staff. Danny was hired as a buser, when in fact they wanted to hide him away from the customers. He had to roll silverware every morning, and at first they told him when he completed enough he would start to bus tables. However, that agreement did not last long. The manager then wanted him to continue to wrap silverware in napkins for the remainder of the time he worked. This was a boring job and one that Danny had difficulty staying focused to completion. He was too hyperactive to stand in one location for three hours wrapping silverware. When I contacted the manager to check on Danny's progress they inferred there was a problem. I then agreed to a meeting to discuss solutions. Their complaints were unfounded, especially a comment suggesting that Danny talked about the manager in a derogatory manner to another employee. This was totally at odds with Danny's character. He never communicated on a personal level with other employees since he never felt enough of a comfort level to do so. That type of accusation could not possibly hold any truth to it. We were dismayed and unsure about the next path to follow. The manager also complained that Danny was a poor employee because he was not completing the required assigned work. He described my son as unable to buss and set tables. This restaurant management had elected to train Danny by themselves but failed to do so. My suggestion was to provide a job coach and they reluctantly agreed. This was my first hint of an employment problem and the need for intervention before they fired him. We felt they intended to fire him at this time.

Danny was provided with a job coach from the Department of Rehabilitation Services (DORS). Danny had been a client since he was eighteen years old, although this was the first time he was in need of their services. This underlines the importance of forging connections and joining organizations that may or may not be needed at the time. Some of these agencies have long waiting lists and if you wait until the service is needed, it might be too late. The only other agency we had joined was to obtain respite care for Danny before he was able to care for himself. The high school he attended had a counselor with direct communication with DORS and we met with them on a yearly basis. This counselor then refers its clients to agencies needed for job placement, job coaches, parent references, and most importantly referrals for students attempting to ease into the community as a whole. If students are planning to attend a workshop instead of securing employment it is of utmost urgency to visit and secure a place on their waiting list at eighteen years of age.

That being said, we thought a job coach could solve the restaurant dilemma. We knew that Danny was happier at the fast food restaurant, but we did not want to put all our eggs in one basket. Managers and employees have a high turnover rate and his situation might not continue to be as idyllic as he felt it was currently. We wanted Danny to have employment choices and skills therefore; we fought to make his busing job to his and his employer's satisfaction.

The coach was wonderful and spent each morning with Danny, much to the restaurant's consternation. She instructed him in setting tables and completing their "much loved" silverware wrapping. As it turned out they had not instructed him at all. Now, the job coach was convinced that he was an excellent employee and could bus as well, if not better than, anyone else. It still was not enough for this group of employers. They invented as many excuses, as they could to not allow Danny to be seen. They had him punch out earlier and earlier so he was not working when the lunch crowd entered. They continued to berate him until I finally wrote them a letter requesting an end to the harassment and discrimination. I reminded them that this was against the law. They were afraid to fire him because they were afraid I would sue them. The area manager called a meeting because I had made him nervous by placing grievances in writing. During this meeting we were basically told that Danny was lucky to have a job and was needed only to wrap silverware. It was then that I learned a lesson that was difficult to swallow. You can force only a limited amount of change. We were able to force them not to fire Danny but we were unable to force them to respect him or even to be nice. We allowed Danny to quit this job, at his own request, and we reminded him that they were mean to all their employees, not just him. This job was damaging to his self-esteem and we were sorry that he had to experience such discrimination. On the other hand, we hoped that each life experience, even difficult ones, helped Danny to grow and mature. Danny never forgot his bad experience, and still reminds us more than five years later when we drive past, not to patronize their establishment.

The manager at his fast food restaurant was thrilled to add as many hours to his schedule as he was capable of working. He began to work a four-day week for a total of twenty-five hours per week. Once again, our only obstacle was transportation. He traveled out of our suburb, causing the bus fare to rise to $5.00 each way. In addition to the cost, the only way this service was available was by calling at 6 a.m. each day to request next day service. This was the only way we would be able to transport Danny to his work site. It seemed impossible at first, but when there is a will, there is a way. My husband and I quickly rose to the occasion and arranged bus transportation on a daily basis. We then stop on our way home, pick him up and drive him home. If we are delayed, Danny has learned to wait patiently and not become too anxious. This is another one of the miracles of development that seemed to arrive just in time. He needed to reduce his feelings of anxiety to function on a daily basis in a work setting complete with unforeseen circumstances that can arise and to travel by himself. Somehow he rose to the occasion.

Danny has worked at this wonderful fast food restaurant for over nine years and continues to enjoy his employment. He works hard at producing French fries for many satisfied customers and has gained smiles from his coworkers as well as their respect. This employment has prompted Danny to continue to grow and mature.

In addition to employment and the transition program, one of the enormous steps Danny took when reaching the age of eighteen was to register to vote. It was with pleasure but with much anxiety that Danny took part in his right and responsibility to vote in a United States election.

This is how it works: We notify the judges when entering the polling place that Danny needs assistance. The ballot is then read to him as needed. He is able to locate the names of certain politicians, but since we did not want him to punch the incorrect name, assistance is the logical way to go. As with anything new, the first time is the hardest. He skips the section for judges and only votes for the offices and candidates he is familiar with from watching television news reports. He would not be the only one not participating in our election process if he was unable to vote, but we feel it is worth going the extra mile to enable him to be a regular voter. After all, his vote counts as much as the rest of the population. There is not a separate vote for the handicapped population and that makes at least this activity equal.

I believe all of these activities in the community have enabled Danny to continue to grow and develop. I believe the scariest revelation we have experienced is identifying other friends of Danny that have regressed since departing from the transition program. A lack of stimulation might be the source of this regression and not one that Danny will have to experience. In many ways, Danny continues to gain both life skills and developmental ones. In his case, he is not too old to continue to learn. I believe that is true for all adults, including myself.

Eighteen years of age is also the signal for parents to outline the future for their child both financially and health wise through legal means. It is a time of assessment and taking stock of past and future plans. The plan to accomplish this is necessary and, although difficult, will protect your child in many ways. I had reservations and experienced nervousness at the mention of a will. That meant to me the need to plan to leave Danny in someone else's care. It was a traumatic awareness that was more than difficult for me to face. Still, I have always tackled what I needed to even if the road was difficult. Raising a child with Fragile X or any other disability calls for strength that most parents are not aware they possess until the situation presents itself. This was the problem I had to tackle now. I made an appointment with a lawyer who traveled throughout the United States assisting parents with their long-term plans. She specialized in writing wills and other documents for parents and their disabled children. Her specialty derived from a need to help others with similar family make-ups. It turned out that her daughter was handicapped also. I am not certain if her daughter was Fragile X, but her abilities were similar to Danny's.

Today there are numerous seminars available to parents to assist them in availing themselves of completing documents to obtain social security benefits. The resources were not available on such a wide scale seven to ten years ago. I had to search for referrals. One great resource was Danny's high school. They had compiled a list of resources and agencies available for assistance. There were workshops, agencies and group homes listed to consider.

We decided to complete a document called "Power of Attorney for Health." That meant that we had determined Danny unable to make a decision concerning his health. We knew that if he ever required surgery or ever was required to sign consent to hospitalize or operate he would impulsively refuse. This is a decision that would have to be made by another responsible adult. We did not declare him incompetent in any other way, but were advised further restrictions would be necessary if we placed him in a group home.

The decision of where to live has to be made. For those lucky enough to attend a transition program, it can be delayed for a few years. For those not attending a transition program, this decision is necessary after high school graduation. For us the decision was a simple one. Danny was employed and was happy at home. We knew that we could provide him with the best quality of life and we had no intention of sharing that responsibility or taking a risk of losing that quality of life by moving him to a group home. As each individual situation varies, it is only possible for Mike and I to detail and describe the best road for us to travel.

If your child had been unsuccessful in the world of work, it is the time to visit workshops. Those are centers where handicapped adults go, usually for forty hours a week, to work. Most of the clients love their daily work and are paid a stipend. It usually amounts to a dollar or two an hour. They complete numerous odd jobs for many different companies including stuffing envelopes and factory-type assembly. Each location is different and the jobs always vary. The adults enjoy the socialization and camaraderie. It is definitely better than staying at home, but is not superior to gainful community employment. One of the downsides is the lack of contact with non-handicapped peers and others in the community.

Chapter Ten:
A Quarter of a Century Later

As we approach Dan's twenty-fifth birthday we cannot help but reflect on the long and exciting journey we traveled to arrive at this moment. We no longer call our son Danny and I cannot recollect exactly the moment the transformation to calling him Dan took place. Actually, it was a gradual occurrence, and a miraculous one at that. How did the years pass so quickly? It seems like just last week that we were celebrating his first birthday with heartfelt thanksgiving at his survival.

Today Dan is healthier than ever. He continues to suffer from asthma and related allergies, but he is thriving. Dan carries his inhaler wherever he leaves the house and does not drink or eat anything that contains milk. He can, however, now tolerate small amounts of cheese. He is over six feet tall and weighs over one hundred and sixty pounds. We joke that it is a good thing that his medicine stunted his growth, or he would have grown to be taller that our doorways. We are immensely happy with his physical development.

Equally important to address is Dan's emotional development that, unfortunately, is not always at an adult level. He has difficulty expressing himself and that still, at times, leads to tantrums and angry words. He is better at expressing his happiness as well as his disappointments at home, but unfortunately, that is also, where his anger is directed. He is under complete control at work and in the community. In fact, his teachers were always surprised when during conferences we interjected this phenomenon. They could not explain why this well- mannered young man would behave differently at home. Dan's home behavior management continues to be an area that we feel needs some work and hopefully will continue to improve with time. He is well behaved and helpful except for these occasional outbursts. His interpersonal relationships and daily community interactions continue to be managed smoothly and without any outbursts or difficulties.

Dan is in charge of many household tasks and is very diligent about completing them. He is in charge of recycling and garbage removal. He never forgets the day before pick up to take everything to the curb. He assists in washing and drying clothes as well as carrying in groceries. Dan reaches for anything I cannot, and completes our family in every possible way.

Currently, Dan works four days a week and is proud of his accomplishments to do so. He wakes early, shaves, dresses, and eats breakfast before we wake. He needs very little sleep, and survives on less than seven hours a night. He is able to take care of himself physically in all ways. Dan does continue to depend upon his routine to feel content as well as relaxed. It continues to be difficult for him to adjust to changes, but now it is not necessary for too many changes to occur. That is a message to all parents. One key to unlocking the door to success for your now adult child is to find what works and stick to it. For Dan it was a job he enjoys and recreation to relax. It is what works that is important and not how long the road was to reach the destination.

Dan continues to participate in special recreation activities as well as watch television, movies, and listen with headphones to music and radio. Every spring Dan trains and participates in Special Olympics. We attend the State Special Olympics each June and love every minute of it. Dan has stayed in the dorms of the college where the Olympics take place for the past fifteen years, and it has been a rewarding as well as a challenging experience in every way. Special Olympics allows each and every athlete to feel special. It is an event that should not be missed.

Dan wears glasses and last year we had a shock when we took Dan to the eye doctor for a routine exam. He was tested for color blindness by being asked to identify letters in a book. During this exam, the letters are camouflaged by colored designs. I was present and suddenly awakened by the realization that Dan no longer reversed the letters identified. I asked the assistant for reassurance, thinking that maybe she had compensated for his reversals. She replied that he had only reversed one letter.

The second shock occurred when Dan was able to read the letters across the eye chart. He was tracking without any assistance. How did this developmental problem that prevented him from reading correct itself so late in life? No one can answer that question for me and it is unimportant in any case. The significance of this development is that it leaves the door open to reading instruction. If Dan is now able to track words and not suffer from too many reversals, there is a possibility that he will soon be able to learn to read. I intend to enroll him in a literacy program. It is never too late to learn and Dan had taught me that his development progresses at his rate not one dictated by others. He has Fragile X syndrome, but I continue to be amazed at his progress and daily success.

We have taken yearly road trips since Dan was three years old. At first, we traveled to destinations within a day or two from our home, but as time passed, we increased the distance and the time traveling. Our favorite destination is Florida. Without sounding like a travel agent, this location has always been the perfect place for us. We loved to sightsee as well as relax at the beach. Dan always loved the pool and had learned to swim before he was ten years old. We visited theme parks and found a wonderful family resort on the ocean where we rented a cottage each summer for more than five years. Each time we returned, Dan enjoyed it more. Three years ago, we purchased a condominium on the beach. Dan has his own room, fully equipped with a radio, headphones and a television set. We will spend our summers there until the day when we retire, when we plan to move to Florida. We envision Dan always living with us, and really could not imagine life without him. He will gradually become more and more comfortable with the move and life in Florida before we move there on a permanent basis. We believe his quality of life could not be any better.

Dan can be recognized by his friendly smile and his classic Fragile X handshake. Dan's complete handshake, outstretched arm, but turned away head and body are a definite sign of his accomplishments, yet a reminder of his birthright.

Today, our son is unlike the broken toy he was identified as by his baby brother so many years past. He has matured and incorporated his pieces to function as a contributing member of our society. We love him dearly and thank God for sending us this special child.

Footnotes and citations

1. National Fragile X Foundation
Website: http://www.FragileX.org
Last visited 6/26/03

2. Conquer Fragile X Inc. Website
Website: http://www.cfxf.org
Last visited 6/26/03

3. National Fragile X Foundation
Website: http://www.FragileX.org
Last visited 6/26/03

4. National Fragile X Foundation
Website: http://www.FragileX.org
Last visited 6/26/03

5. Failure to Thrive - a term commonly used to describe younger children who are not gaining weight normally. Children with failure to thrive usually have a weight that is below the 3rd to 5th percentile for their age and a declining growth velocity (meaning they are not gaining weight as expected) and/or a shift downward in their growth percentiles, crossing two or more percentiles on their growth charts.

6. Projectile vomiting - when your baby brings up the stomach contents in a forceful way. The amount of milk or food can seem large on the floor, but is usually the amount of the last feed. Babies may projectile vomit occasionally, but if it happens two or three times a day, see your doctor.

7. TAY-SACHS disease (TSD) - a fatal genetic disorder in children that causes progressive destruction of the central nervous system.
The disease is named for Warren Tay (1843-1927), a British ophthalmologist who in 1881 described a patient with a cherry-red spot on the retina of the eye. It is also named for Bernard Sachs (1858-1944), a New York neurologist whose work several years later

provided the first description of the cellular changes in Tay-Sachs disease. Sachs also recognized the familial nature of the disorder, and, by observing numerous cases, he noted that most babies with Tay-Sachs disease were of eastern European Jewish origin.

8. EEG -the electroencephalogram (EEG) is a registration on paper of the electrical potential differences between electrodes on the scalp as a function of time. Neurologists use EEGs to study and classify the state of the brain. For example, the EEG shows a characteristic rhythm of about 10 cycles per second when we are awake, at rest and with our eyes closed. This rhythm is called the "alpha rhythm". Epilepsy (see below) is a disease of the brain. During an epileptic seizure, the EEG looks very different, and due to the characteristic shape of the curves in the signal they are described as "spike waves". Under both conditions, EEGs were recorded and band-pass filtered (0.1 - 75 Hz) using standard equipment at the University Hospital,
van Erp, M. (1988).

PhD thesis, University of Leiden, Leiden, The Netherlands.

9. Epilepsy - a physical condition that occurs when there is a sudden, brief change in how the brain works. When brain cells are not working properly, a person's consciousness, movement, or actions may be altered for a short time. These physical changes are called epileptic seizures. Epilepsy is therefore sometimes called a seizure disorder. Epilepsy affects people in all nations and of all races.
(Epilepsy Foundation of America-National Office 4351 Garden City Drive, Suite 406Landover, MD 20785)

10. Petite-mal – this type of seizure falls into the category of an absence seizure. The seizure can occur frequently, it can cause unconsciousness, however recovery occurs quickly. Oftentimes, this type of seizure goes unnoticed, which can create learning issues for the child who is "spacing off" during classroom time.

11. Urinary reflux- urinary reflux describes when urine moves from the bladder back up into the kidney (i.e. goes in the opposite direction than it should). Reflux happens because the valves at the ends of

the ureters (the tubes which connect the kidney with the bladder) malfunction

12. Hyperactivity - A maladaptive and abnormal increase in activity that is inconsistent with developmental levels. Includes frequent fidgeting, inappropriate running, excessive talking, and difficulty in engaging in quiet activities

13. Laryngoscopy - examination of the interior of the larynx (voice box) with either the aid of a small mirror held against the back of the palate (indirect) or a rigid or flexible viewing tube called a laryngoscope (direct).

14. Radionuclide cystogram - A radionuclide cystogram is a test (nuclear scan) using radioactive material (radioisotope) that is placed into the bladder. A scanner then detects radioactivity.

15. Ritalin (Methylphenidate)- Methylphenidate is a medication prescribed for individuals (usually children) who have an abnormally high level of activity or attention-deficit hyperactivity disorder (ADHD). According to the National Institute of Mental Health, about 3 to 5 percent of the general population has the disorder, which is characterized by agitated behavior and an inability to focus on tasks. Methylphenidate also is occasionally prescribed for treating narcolepsy.

16. Cylert (Pemoline) - is a drug used to treat attention-deficit-disorder in children. This drug is from a family of drugs known as central nervous system stimulants. Originally used in older persons to improve cognitive functioning.

17. Non-categorical- not specified

18. Tactile defensiveness- a specific type of sensory defensiveness, or hyperarousal. Tactile defensiveness means that the person overreacts to touch and may refuse or avoid touching. About 60-90% of boys

with fragile X and some girls with the full mutation are described as having tactile defensiveness.

19. Hyper-arousal- a state of elevated or increased alertness, awareness or wakefulness.

20. Hypo-arousal- a state of lessened or decreased alertness, awareness or wakefulness.

21. Cross-over ability – the ability to move from one side of the body to the other with arms, legs, hands, eyes, etc. (requires communication between left and right hemispheres of the brain.

22. Adrenaline shot- a shot of the chemical Adrenaline or Kenalog often given to people with asthma to stimulate normal breathing.

23. Nebulizer- a mechanical (electrical) air compressor used to deliver asthma medication.

24. IEP- Individualized Educational Plan.

25. Respite Care- provides families with specialized temporary child care.

26. Gag Reflex- response to posterior pharynx tactile stimulation causing an individual to gag.

27. Workshops- sheltered workshops allow the mentally challenged to learn job skills and get used to work routines, with the goal of preparing workers for eventual placement in regular jobs.

28. Group Homes- an institution that promotes the self-sufficient and independent living of individuals with mental disabilities. By experiencing life with other people and by supporting one another in daily life activities, mentally challenged individuals can lead independent lives.

29. Transition Program – a program that assists high school graduates with disabilities to achieve positive transition to the community.

30. CGG Expansion - genetic mutation found in fragile X syndrome

31. FMR1 Gene – Fragile X Mental retardation 1 Gene.

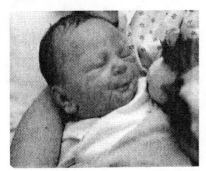

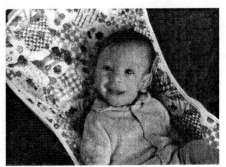

Danny Morgan at 4 days old. He seemed carefree.

At 10 weeks old, the left side of Danny's face was clearly flat

A survivor at 5 months.

Danny at 7 months on the road to recovery.   Danny at 1 year old.

Danny had many happy moments at age two.

Between the ages of three and four Danny developed a winning smile.

Danny now had a little brother.

Danny at age 5 before going
trick or treating on Halloween

Danny playing next to his brother in the sandbox.

Hand flapping is still evident

Dan loved Snoopy, but he was still ready to escape.

"Batman is so cool!"

Danny with his medals at the Special Olympics

All dressed up for his brother's Bar Mitzvah.

Dan's first dog, Annie.

Marching in the Special Olympics Parade.

On a family vacation in New York.

Celebrating with his teammates at the state Special Olympics.

Having a blast at his 25th birthday party with the family.

Relaxing in Florida.   "The Winner!"

Dan "chilling" with Grandma and Grandpa,

Su 52 Michael Sp D,

Dear Peter,

Hi! We hope you enjoyed a good Valentine's Day! Cheri brought over heart shaped donuts & Cars Valentines with car character pencils. I gave John a "Cars" DVD I had been given by Cheri & Mary. I gave Jim a "Cars" color book & paint set. He likes to paint little cars & his bike trailer. I got dad the CD "Presidents & Prophets" about our church prophets relationship with different US Presidents. I got Cheri & Mary the book Semplify + as well the gift certificate. Your Valentine package is in the mail.

Jim flew to his mom's Valentine Day's morn. I was planning to go too but I hadn't found coverage for John & James for Saturday. I finally called Pres. Perry & Brother Roberts. Pres Perry said he could stop by at regular intervals. Bro Roberts said he could come by & stay 9am till Dad got home about 5:15pm. We chose Bro Roberts yet were so thankful for Bro Perry's offer too!

After arrangements were made Shawn's mom helped me check bus & train schedules on her computer. Bro Perry told us that Tiches, 2 doors down on Princess, next to McCormac's have moved out & plan to rent. We called & they want $850 which is what they pay where they are now. Shawn & his mom plan to meet with Tiches Sat am.

I planned to take the 10pm Greyhound & use Red Line to get there. Cheri said I needed to catch the 7:55 Red Line. That was my plan. Then I loaded my boys in the car at & general at Radar & Main. I waited for Cheri to bring Jim by with his Tonka toy. Jim had the key & was happy to help but he had cut himself shaving & was bleeding all over! He didn't complain he just said oh I was shaving! I was quite alarmed! Jim insisted on riding in Cheri's car with her to her place to get some ice. I rushed home!

About The Author

Marilyn Morgan is an inspirational parent, educator, and advocate for her child. She possesses a wisdom gained form years of experience raising a special needs child. During her 30 years of experience as a public school teacher, with a Master's degree in Education, she has utilized inclusion methods for developmentally-delayed and behavior disorder students, as well as, attended many Individual Education Plan (IEP) conferences.

She has struggled since her Fragile X child's birth to find educational, medical and social resources to meet her son's needs. Today's parents are no longer alone. Marilyn Morgan answers the question, "what do I do now?"

Deeper Shuttle was waiting in the drive way. I called them while I was looked at f my car, when I realized it was too late for Red Line. I explained to the Shuttle that I couldn't leave now as my son had just cut himself + might have to go to the emergency room. It was a woman driver. She was very nice. She said, Don't worry I am a mom too. Take care of your son + if you want me to come back later I will.

At the same time, Mary who helps as she just get off work, I told her about Jenn She needed to her house to check on him, She came back with him very calm. Its a small scratch across the upper lip. She put a bag of frozen vegtables on it She reminded me that face wounds always bleed alot, she showed her Montessori teacher calm + experience.

Printed in the United States
49892LVS00005B/430-480